The Whole-Hearted Healing™ Workbook

Volume 1
First Edition

By Paula Courteau

Foreword by Dr. Grant McFetridge

Institute for the Study of Peak States

The Whole-Hearted Healing™ Workbook, Volume 1, Copyright 2012 by Paula Courteau. All rights reserved. Published in Canada. No part of this book may be used or reproduced in any manner whatsoever without written permission of the Institute for the Study of Peak States Press, except in the case of brief quotations embodied in critical articles and reviews.

First Edition
First Printing, 2012

Library and Archives Canada Cataloguing in Publication

Courteau, Paula, 1960- The whole-hearted healing workbook / by Paula Courteau ; foreword by Grant McFetridge. -- 1st ed.

Includes bibliographical references and index. ISBN 978-0-9734680-3-8 (v. 1)

1. Regression (Psychology)--Therapeutic use--Popular works. 2. Peak experiences--Popular works. I. Institute for the Study of Peak States II. Title.

RC489.R42C69 2012 615.8'51 C2012-905846-7

Published simultaneously in Danish under the title "*Healing med hjertet: En introduktion til Whole-Hearted Healing™*".

All quotes and adaptations from *The Basic Whole-Hearted Healing™ Manual* by Grant McFetridge and Mary Pellicer, *Peak States of Consciousness: Theory and Applications* by Grant McFetridge and *Triune Brain Therapy* by Monti Scribner are by kind permission of the authors and of the Institute for the Study of Peak States Press.

Some of the material in this book appeared previously in a slightly different form in the Institute for the Study of Peak States Newsletters, published on-line by ISPS.

"Whole-Hearted Healing™," the "Laks Peak Experience to State Tech-nique™," "Triune Brain Therapy™," the "Crosby Vortex Technique™," the "Courteau Projection Technique™," and the "Silent Mind Technique™" are trademarks of the Institute for the Study of Peak States.

Institute for the Study of Peak States Press
3310 Cowie Road
Hornby Island, British Columbia
V0R 1Z0 Canada
http://www.peakstates.com

Table of Contents

Foreword

I am absolutely delighted with this opportunity to recommend this book. It fills a real need in our Institute's work. It is a useful, readable and practical self-help guide, written for the lay public, on a foundation technique in our work with peak states of consciousness, specific disease processes, and pre- and sub-cellular phenomena.

A teacher's greatest ambition is to see his students become enthusiastic about the material and build on what was taught. Paula shares with you her passion and attention to detail, and an original and very important contribution of her own — her projection healing technique. This technique alone is worth the price of this book.

Many excellent therapies have been developed in the last decade, each with their advantages and disadvantages. For example, I generally tell my students to try certain other therapies first (like EFT, TAT, or EMDR) because for many people and situations they are simpler, faster and less painful. However, WHH usually works even when other therapies get stuck — and in this business it's very good to have a reliable alternative.

Basic WHH is an essential technique in learning from the inside what trauma is and how it affects us. WHH also forms the foundation for our more advanced healing techniques, and is also key to our many peak state processes.

-Dr. Grant McFetridge,
The Institute for the Study of Peak States
Hornby Island, BC, Canada

Acknowledgments

This has been a long, wild road. I've had all sorts of help along the way and cannot possibly list each treasure that landed right before me at exactly the right moment. Here, however, are a few of the messengers who stand out.

I want to thank Monti Scribner, first; she was, like me, an Institute student who quite suddenly found herself in the role of an instructor and support person for others. Monti graciously allowed me to use her Triune Brain workshop exercises, and surprised me by also sending a trove of wisdom about the outline I'd written, essentially setting the tone for this book and its future companions. Monti suggested that I use a gradual approach, with lots of exercises, rather than jump right away into using Whole-Hearted Healing. Her presence permeates the structure of this book. (Monti also has the best telephone voice in the universe.)

Next there was novelist Janey Bennett, who treated me to good coffee, cello music and wonderful conversations about peak states and the nature of good writing. Some of these pages will still make her cringe, I'm sure, but it would have been much worse without you, Janey!

The people who taught me, and shared their results, and argued and carried on about this crazy quest, stand out in my mind. In particular, the long-time Institute members who attended the retreat on Hornby Island in May 2002: Dr. Mary Pellicer, Maureen Chandler, Wes Gietz, and our deeply missed, the late Dr. Adam Waisel. We do most of our team work on the phone and online, and many of us had never met. There was something irreplaceable in those few days of intensive work and companionship. Some of these people have gone on to other projects, but each stands as a role model and mentor.

Reaching further back to the very seeds of teaching... to both my parents, who've had their turn doing it, and especially my mother, Monique Courteau, who made teaching her vocation, in and out of the classroom. Some things are bred in the bone, but witnessing a lifetime of intelligent thought, as I did with both my father and mother, sure helps.

Then there were my students: each one of them taught me something. Their stories are all over this book. I didn't set out to teach; I began teaching because they asked me to. I am still teaching because they continue to ask me to. Why else?

Dr. Mary Pellicer, again, and Dr. Laura Chalfin, checked my assumptions and statements about medications and diabetes, volunteering their expertise.

Another bouquet of thanks to Tal Laks for checking the contents of the whole manuscript and adding welcome comments, tips and anecdotes, making this book less of a monologue and more of a conversation; and to John Heinegg, who agreed to proof-read this manuscript for me. Any errors you find happened after the book left his hands.

And finally, the brain behind it all: friend, mentor, slave-driver and accomplice, the Institute's founder and driving force, the maddest and sanest of us all: Grant McFetridge, of course. Thank you. It's been a hell of a road.

Liability Agreement and Safety Warnings

This manual is written primarily for workshop students who are learning the process over several days. We're also making it available for interested laypeople and professionals who are interested in learning the nuts and bolts of the basic Whole-Hearted Healing process.

In a workshop setting, we can supervise and assist you full-time, and remain in contact afterwards. If you intend to use this book for self-study, be aware that these processes are potentially dangerous. If you are not willing to be *totally* responsible for how you use this material, and for any consequences of doing so, than we require that you refrain from using the processes in this book.

It is possible that you will feel extreme distress, both short and long term, if you use the processes in this book. As with any intense psychological process, life-threatening problems might occur due to the possibility of stressing a weak heart, from activating suicidal feelings, triggering latent mental or physical illnesses, and other causes. The research into regression techniques as they relate to deep changes in consciousness is still very young. Although we've explicitly indicated in the text the specific problems you might encounter using these processes, the possibility exists that you may encounter a problem we haven't seen before. You may experience serious or life-threatening problems with any of the processes in this book. The possibility that you may die from using these processes *does* exist.

Given all the above, the following statements constitute a legal agreement between us. Please read the following carefully:

1) The author, any people associated with the Institute for the Study of Peak States, and other contributors to this text cannot and will not take responsibility for what you do with these techniques.

2) You are required to take complete responsibility for your own emotional and physical well-being if you use these processes or any variations of them.

3) You are required to instruct others on whom you use these processes, or variations of these processes, that they are completely responsible for their own emotional and physical well-being.

4) Use these techniques under the supervision of a qualified therapist or physician as appropriate.

5) You must agree to hold harmless the author and anyone associated with this text or with the Institute for the Study of Peak States from any claims made by anyone, yourself included, on whom you use these processes, or variations of them.

6) Many of the process names in this book are trademarked, and so the usual legal restrictions apply to their public use.

Continuing with this text constitutes a legal agreement to these conditions. Thank you for your understanding.

Several years ago, my friend Paula Vibert returned home from a long retreat to find her favourite cat dying. The cat had taken no food or drink for several days. He was emaciated, drooling and incontinent. Paula's husband and children had made a nest of blankets in a basket, but everyone was reluctant to touch the poor, smelly bag of bones. Paula was saddened at this rejection and reflected that if she were the one dying, she would want contact and acceptance, no matter how she looked. So each day, she spent some time holding her cat, on a towel in her lap.

Soon, she noticed an unforeseen pattern. After sitting in her lap for a while, the cat looked more alive. After a day or two he started to drink. Then to eat. Then to walk.

The cat regained about ninety percent of his previous state of health. We do not know how, but we know this: Paula did not set out to heal her cat. Her only agenda was to spend time in love and acceptance. *And when she spent enough time doing this,* something else happened.

Introduction

One good morning in the year 2000, I decided to live with an open heart.

Some new hope of love had crumbled into grief — again — but this time I asked, What if I were to keep on loving, no matter what, rather than following my usual modus, which was to close myself behind a hard shell, to hide behind the battlements? What if I were to keep on loving, whenever possible, with no other agenda in mind?

I had no idea what this really meant. Knew in principle that one can have an open heart and still stay safe, but didn't know how it was done.

So I started living on a wing and a prayer, careening between fear and love, but committed to feeling, to being, to accepting.

Six months into this quest, completely by chance, I met Grant McFetridge.

I have no background in any of the thousands of alternative therapies on the market, so his stories, coming from someone so used to navigating the unseen, stretched my beliefs to capacity. But hadn't I decided to keep an open heart? And did this not dictate that I listen through before judging or rejecting? I'd had my share of mystical visions, serendipitous coincidences and unexplainable experiences, after all, so I held my peace rather than casting stones at the mirror. There was logic here too, a structure that had the potential to help me make sense of those strangest moments of my life, and I was intrigued enough to check out the website of the Institute for the Study of Peak States.

I read a paper about a regression therapy. I had never tried such a thing, but knew other people who had, with mixed results. In fact, mixed results seemed to be a feature of most alternative healing techniques. The paper, at least, seemed to discuss that particular issue openly and suggested some solutions. One of them sprang from this observation: we usually see ourselves as outside our body when we perceive a trauma image of ourselves in the past. Another had to do with our expectations of what it feels like when a problem is completely resolved. Essentially, Grant had discovered that many trauma techniques don't work when people stay dissociated while they try to heal; people who spontaneously stay in their bodies are the ones who get textbook success. Grant also realized that the most drastic changes happen when one keeps healing beyond the point of merely feeling reconciled with the past event. In other words, most regression therapies don't keep at it long enough. This seemed to make good sense, so I took up the paper's challenge and tried the technique. I found myself at a traumatic moment shortly after my birth—wanting the breast, getting a bottle instead. Healed the trauma completely. Lost the strong gag reflex that had made it so difficult to brush my teeth! *That* was unexpected. I was hooked.

I did one session with Grant to overcome a problem about feeling my way into my pre-birth universe. I'll return to this later, but it was, a year or so later, the topic of one of my first amendments to the third edition of *The Basic Whole-Hearted Healing Manual.* Before very long, I was immersed in the editing of training materials.

I'm not much of a joiner. I like to do things my own way and without witnesses. Especially emotional work! I continued solo, using the website and the manual's second edition. But I stayed in touch with Grant, calling him with my questions.

The pre-birth world is fascinating. It felt — it *still* feels — like being an explorer on the moon, a moon populated with my own tribe of ghosts. And daily life was getting easier all the time... The problems I'd healed really weren't coming back!

I started to experience... peak states. Those things the Institute is named after. A peak experience —Abraham Maslow coined these terms — is a wonderful, perfect moment. Maslow catalogued all kinds of different ones, from moments of perfect peace or happiness to very spiritual feelings of unity with the universe or strange communions with other consciousnesses. A peak state is a peak experience that lasts, and lasts... and lasts. Well, I started getting those. Peace. Freedom from past traumas. An underlying happiness that serves as a ground or canvas for everything else I feel. The perception of the universe as a field of infinite possibility.

One day, at the end of a session, I felt as if my whole skin was falling off in slabs! Since then, it doesn't feel like I have skin at all: it feels like my boundary is made of vapour, and almost nothing other people do ever feels personal to me.

My life changed completely. So this is what it's like to live without trauma? And what about that open-heart thing? I found I didn't have to consciously try anymore: love and compassion flowed naturally, as if I were hard-wired for them.

It's only after using the technique for a couple of years that I started reading the literature and finding out what others in the field had done. I needed more background knowledge before I felt comfortable enough to teach. I was gratified to find many regression accounts that were similar to mine. I was doubly gratified to realize how rapid, comparatively speaking, my own progress had been.

In these pages I quote both Stanislav Grof, the father of Holotropic Therapy, and Arthur Janov, of *Primal Scream* fame, not despite the fact that they vigorously disagree with each other, but because of it. Their common ground is wider than their rivalry would lead to believe. Each side of their scholarly chasm shares ground with our work as well: Janov uses the triune brain model but did not believe that one could remember experiences before birth, until his own patients somehow hammered it home to him. Only his later books reflect this aspect, and even there, all the examples recount birth experiences. He still tends to lump earlier experiences in the realm of delusion. Grof, on the other hand, sees no limit to how far one can regress, but his dismissal of the triune brain theory means that his clients' projections go unchallenged and unresolved, hence the complex menagerie of spirits and archetypes they end up having to contend with. Both Grof and Janov are well worth reading. They are pioneers in this field and have had access to much wider resources than does our little Institute. Their work blazed the trail for ours, and their medical findings further validate the evidence from our own case studies.

So far, *The Basic Whole-Hearted Healing Manual,* now in its third edition, had been the only reference book on our regression healing method. It is designed as a workshop manual, mostly with professional therapists in mind. But since I started teaching Whole-Hearted Healing, I've seen a growing need for a do-it-yourself trauma-healing resource. Our Institute uses WHH mainly as a research tool, but each basic teaching session reminds me of its relevance as an easy-to-learn technique to heal past traumas. WHH is portable; you need no equipment, no therapist, no special room. All you need is time, a bit of privacy, and the willingness to re-experience some very strange chunks of your past.

Due to its short history, I know of few people who've used WHH long term; for that reason, many of the examples in this book are from my own session notes. I've also used some of my students' sessions. As much as possible, I chose beginners' stories; the problems in them can be resolved with the skill set you'll acquire with this book. Out of concern for my students' privacy, I've shamelessly dreamed up names, and sometimes even made gender swaps and combined stories so nobody can tell who's who. I'm especially careful because a few of my students and clients live here on my small island, where maintaining any kind of privacy is a tall order. I am grateful to all those who lent me their stories.

How to Use this Book

This workbook started as a collection of reminders and worksheets for my students. I fleshed these out, quoting at times from Grant and Mary's *Basic Whole-Hearted Healing Manual*; then I added some brand-new material drawn from my own interests and explorations: the projection exercise, my own version of healing dualities, dream-work, and some of the material on mixing techniques. Here and there I interspersed thoughts on my favourite topic: the implications of doing in-depth personal exploration as a way of life or as a personal discipline. Later on, Tal Laks (a student of Dr. Adam Waisel and the Institute's most experienced healer and teacher after Grant) and Grant read the first draft and added a wealth of comments and anecdotes, which I preserved almost verbatim, whether they agreed with my text or not. This added another layer of teaching; Grant and Tal's experiences became sub-plots of this volume, the monologue turned into a conversation; and the occasional contradictions merely underscore the newness of all this material. The book is also my sneaky way of getting my own experience on paper, a disguised memoir, and I hope it can become a companion on your healing road.

Workshops and coaching are still the best ways to learn this technique. But workshops last a few days, and what do we retain? This book can be part of the answer: a synopsis, a reminder, a trouble-shooting guide. In this context, you may pick through it piecemeal, as the need arises. If you're fresh from a workshop, you might wish to skip the exercises in chapter 2 (the Prerequisites), but the theory sections of that chapter are still likely to hold some useful information for you. I've also tried to include as many ways as possible to search topics and trouble-shoot problems; so in addition to a detailed table of contents and index, you will find two trouble-shooting charts: a general one with common questions (appendix E), and also a chart of special occurrences (appendix D). I've also provided ample margins for annotations.

If you're a determined newcomer, you can learn WHH from scratch through this book. The exercises in Chapter 2 touch on each component of the process. If you take the time to try them, your first healing won't be nearly as intimidating because you will already be familiar with each element. You *must*, however, agree to take responsibility for your own adventures in consciousness. See the liability agreement on page 13.

Some students who have taken our workshops will notice a difference of emphasis in the way this book approaches regression. That is because the workshop instructors, for the most part, have the ability to regress at will and to perceive trauma sequences in their entirety; that point of view informs their vocabulary and their way of teaching. Also, the workshops are conceived for healing professionals, so there is a much greater emphasis on the need to see and identify past images. This book, on the other hand, assumes no special ability on the student's part; the goals of personal healing and exploration are more modest, and therefore the method is based on recognizing and accepting the perceptual gifts that we do have, and using them at their fullest. The ability to regress into the far past develops over time, as our subconscious learns to feel safe in these strange landscapes.

People often think that techniques that only involve the mind and emotions are intrinsically safe. It's all in my head; what could possibly go wrong?

I wish it were so. But delving into old traumas can stir up unconscious material that is extremely uncomfortable. Sooner or later, if you start healing yourself, your *big one* will show up. Your core trauma, a central issue, in defence of which you've organized your whole life. When some of this trauma remains incompletely healed at the end of a session, the issue can seem quite immediate and overwhelming. In extreme cases we've seen clients become suicidal. The answer, of course is... more healing. When we finish healing traumas with Whole-Hearted Healing, only calm, peace and a light, weightless feeling remain. Thus, it is your responsibility to continue to heal until the trauma is resolved. It is also your responsibility to get help from a local help line, or a counsellor or psychotherapist in your area, if you're extremely distressed or suicidal.

In workshops, students team up as 'healing buddies,' and are encouraged to maintain that relationship after they go home. Learning from this book with a healing buddy, if it's possible, simply makes sense. A traveling companion, or several: someone to compare notes with and trade stories with, and someone who will check on you when you approach something heavy. Someone to hold your hand and remind you to stay in your body. Someone who can call for help if things seem out of hand. It's worth considering.

Occasionally, radical transformations and amazing transpersonal experiences occur with this work. All of them are safe: they are our birthright; they are how we're supposed to be. But some people feel fear and discomfort when such experiences first appear. The most drastic and sudden change for me, so far, was the moment when I felt a sensation of 'skin' slipping off my body. I was immediately comfortable with my new peak state, but others who healed the same events felt naked and vulnerable. Again the answer is—yes, more healing. All the strange peak states and experiences we encounter through the advanced stages of this work are intrinsically comfortable and natural. Any discomfort is due to trauma. If you get into a new state of being that feels overwhelming, the Spiritual Emergency Network or a Whole-Hearted Healing practitioner are your best bets for help. See appendix D for resources. See also Grant's book *Peak States of Consciousness, Volume 1* for more details about those types of experiences.

Medications and WHH

In most cases, you can use Whole-Hearted Healing even if you're taking medications for physical or psychiatric conditions. In fact, discontinuing your medication could put you in serious danger.

Our experience, and that of others using power therapies, shows, in particular, that neither lithium nor selective serotonin reuptake inhibitors (SSRIs, such as Paxil and Prozac) will interfere with the regression process. You can, and should, stay on your medication while doing the therapy.[1]

Grant's *Basic Whole-Hearted Healing Manual* states that the tricyclic antidepressant desipramine can block people from regressing. I should clarify here that this problem showed up in a client who was using the medication at full dose. Nowadays, with the advent of SSRIs, physicians typically prescribe desipramine and other tricyclic antidepressants for chronic pain rather than for depression. The bedtime dose for pain control is only about a tenth of the antidepressant dose and is unlikely to

[1] See, among others, Gerald D. French and Chrys J. Harris, *Traumatic Incident Reduction,* pp. 126-127. The authors also caution about tricyclic antidepressants (see next paragraph in the text) and speculate that "any drug that tends to have either a sedative effect or a tendency to create euphoria will interfere with the efficacy of TIR at least to some degree." We have shown, however, that it's fully possible to regress and heal effectively even with a somewhat narrowed emotional range. Don't quit your medication.

block access to past emotions.[2] If in doubt, see the section on working with a narrow emotional range in Chapter 3.

Here are some more recent findings from the past director of our Addictions Project, Matthew Fox, about another class of medications that slow down or stall WHH. Matthew writes:

> Valium (Diazepam), Klonopin, Xanax, Ativan (Lorazepam), Librium, and some others are from a class of drugs known as benzodiazepines, which act as a central nervous system depressant. In other words, they slow down the activity of the central nervous system. Many alcoholics substitute benzodiazepines for alcohol because they work in the same way. Benzos are supposed to be used on an 'as-needed' basis, for panic attacks and general anxiety disorders. Or they can be used daily on a temporary basis until other anti-depressant medications can kick in. However, many psychiatrists and MDs write prescriptions for up to 3 and 4 times per day without consideration for addiction and withdrawal problems. Withdrawal from benzos without medical supervision can result in serious side effects such as seizures and death.
>
> I have had the unfortunate experience of trying EFT with people on benzos — in the first case, the client felt great when she left the office, but was overwhelmed with emotions about an hour later, and the effect lasted for about a week. In another case, the client felt nothing during the treatment, but slowly began to feel much better. He then decided he didn't need his Xanax, so he threw them out, which resulted in a serious withdrawal problem and subsequent return of his anxiety. When I have tried WHH on clients who are taking benzos, either the results are unusually slow or the client can't get it together enough emotionally to focus on the intervention. I don't like to use either WHH or EFT on clients while they are taking benzos, and advise them to talk to their doctors about getting off them. [3]

Matthew's experience underlines the additional danger involved with medications and power therapies: the temptation to simply throw out the medication when we feel the first improvements.

If your condition improves, please ask the prescribing physician for a reassessment before discontinuing medication. *Do not discontinue your medication without supervision.* Besides the type of problem Matthew describes, we've also seen a few instances where the main symptoms of a

---

[2] The same cautions would apply to the other medications of the same family: imipramine, amitriptyline and nortriptyline. (Info from Dr. Laura Chalfin.)

[3] Matthew Fox, personal communication.

psychiatric illness resolved, but the principal condition masked a secondary problem that had also been controlled by the medication.

A special caution applies if you have diabetes: Whole-Hearted Healing sessions can use up a surprising amount of blood glucose! It's like an emotional and mental workout rolled into one. So if you are diabetic and tend to easily get hypoglycemic, please monitor your glucose levels carefully. I recommend that you set a timer during your first sessions to remind yourself to check your glucose at least every hour, until you've figured out the pattern. Keep in mind that sessions can greatly differ in mental and emotional intensity; monitor a cross-section of them before letting your guard down. If necessary, have some juice or snacks on hand; you can take a few bites or sips from time to time without breaking the flow of the session.

Chapter 1

Whole-Hearted Healing Memory Aids

This section is a quick overview of the Whole-Hearted Healing process. If you're new at this, it will give you an idea of what we actually do. Please read the 'Prerequisites' in chapter 2 and the more detailed discussion of the process in chapter 3 before starting. Once you're familiar with the process, come back to this section to recap. I suggest you keep the book open at this section during your first solo trip in the past.

The steps will make sense, hopefully, without any other training. The 'Special Situations' section will probably look like insane jargon until you've read more and done some exploration of your own. I simply wanted to keep the two parts together early in the book, ready to be consulted in the heat of the action.

WHH - The Very Very Short Version:

1- Feel it: find the emotion. Where is it in your body? Keep feeling the emotion and body sensation.
2- Stay in your body.
3- Love yourself.

4- Stay in the discomfort through all its transformations, as you go further and further back in time. Continue long enough—until you feel calm, peaceful and light and your issue no longer holds any charge.

WHH: The Steps

Step 1: Find something that's bothering you in the present. Get yourself worked up about it. Write down how you feel, and a few words about what makes you feel that way.

Step 2: Magnify the emotion if you can. Where does it sit in your body? Or: if you are starting from a body sensation, magnify that. What's the emotion inside it?

Step 3: Recall other times when you felt exactly this way. It won't necessarily be the same kind of incident; you're looking for the same type of emotion and body sensation. Choose the earliest incident you can recall, even if it doesn't seem to make logical sense.

Step 4: Place your hand on your chest to remind yourself to stay inside your body. If you see yourself 'out there', merge with the image of yourself until there's only one 'you'. This is the most important step. If this is difficult, try the 'Loving Yourself' technique. Bring the image to yourself and put it on like a sweater. Relaxing your diaphragm, throat and jaw also helps.

Step 5: Love yourself in this moment in the past. Stay in the moment, focusing on any physical area that seems injured, feeling the emotion and the body sensations, with no agenda to change anything. Love yourself exactly as you are. Relive this frozen moment from your past.

Step 6: Stay in this moment until something changes. Often a few words will pop out, having to do with the beliefs that you anchored in that trauma moment. Another emotion may arise, or an earlier situation may arise. Repeat Steps 4, 5 and 6 for the new emotion/body sensation. It doesn't matter if you don't know the story or if you don't know where you are; feel the emotion, feel where it is in your body, love yourself. Keep going further and further back in time this way.

Step 7: When nothing is left except calm, peace and a weightless sensation, you are done. If the moment you healed is before birth, you should also feel large and bright. Stay in the moment for a few minutes, to make sure no further trauma arises. If one does, go back to Step 4.

Step 8: Check your work. There should be no out-of-body image when you look back at the traumatic moment. Look at the description you wrote at the start of the process—it should no longer trigger you. If any emotions besides calm, peace and lightness are present, return to Step 4 or plan to return at a later session.

Special Situations

It is common to encounter one or two of these special situations in each session. Each one is discussed in more detail in chapter 4.

Emptiness or blank feeling

Where in your body is the emptiness or blankness? Move your attention into it. Love yourself for being empty or blank. Be the blank. The hidden emotion will soon arise. Heal it the usual way. Some people get a brief image of the traumatic moment when they press a hand gently into the blank area. Often, going into the sensation of emptiness reveals a hole (see next paragraph).

Holes

A more dramatic version of the 'emptiness' above. Move your attention into the hole. Feel and heal from the perspective of the inside of the hole. Pay special attention to the physical sensations. The emotions often are quite strong once you get past the empty feeling. At the moment when you feel this will *never* go away, you're actually about two thirds of the way through. Stay with the sensations until only calm is left and the hole vanishes.

'New' physical pain

Physical pain sometimes arises seemingly from nowhere during healing. Or chronic pain starts acting up unexpectedly. 'New' pain in this context means 'new in this session'; you may have felt it before. This may be from an earlier event that has not appeared in the picture yet. Or is it a distraction? Magnify the pain, and relax into it rather than trying to avoid it. Do this until you feel the emotion inside the pain. Figure out if it belongs with the problem by thinking back to the trigger. Which injury seems most relevant? Which injury seems earliest? Go with the earliest, the most relevant to the trigger, the most intense. Then heal the emotion and physical sensation in the usual way.

Copies

If it seems like the emotion or physical sensation in your body has the tone of someone else (usually one of your parents or grandparents), release this 'copy' by asking yourself what *you* are feeling at that moment. This will often greatly speed up a 'stuck' healing.

Soul stealing

Sensorially, it is like a pumped-up version of copying, although the cause is different. Voices, emotions, or body sensations clearly coming from somebody else seem to haunt you. Find the emotional tone of the intruding sensation. Make a womb or bubble of it around yourself: surround yourself completely with the sensation. Then move your attention into your lower belly. Love yourself for surviving, for hanging on to this sensation in order to survive. The soul piece often releases suddenly, with the sensation of something whooshing away or a sudden, tiny memory loss: "Who was this person again?"

Soul loss

Rarely, at the end of a session to heal soul loss you might still feel a sensation of loss or lack or flatness; it is often centred in the chest. The feeling will disappear on its own in a few hours, but you can resolve the problem instantly by singing the very first melody that pops into your mind. The lack vanishes within a few minutes of singing.

Pretend-identities

You find yourself in disguise: looking like a lizard, say, or an evil monster, or your grandmother, or an ugly bug, or a block of wood; or else pretending to be your favourite character in a novel or your favourite childhood dream, or just about anything. Stay in your body, love yourself as you are, until the hidden emotion and body sensation arise. Heal these in the usual way.

Archetypal images

Similar to pretend-identities. They often look more intimidating because they're outside your body. You might encounter the monster in the basement, the goddess Diana, an Aztec god that rips out hearts, an immense standing stone, the devil incarnate. Don't worry: it's you. Merge with it. Love yourself as the monster in the basement, or the goddess Diana, or whatever you are. Scan your body for new emotions and sensations. Heal as usual.

Generational traumas

Look for those anytime a trauma feels really, really personal; the trauma feels like it's who you are at the very core, one of your building blocks. You might see or sense a row of people, or a spiral of people, or as a dim row of playing cards or dominoes. Bring to yourself the person who is furthest away from you. Merge with him or her. Feel his or her emotions and body sensations, just as if they were your own. Love yourself as this person. Stay until the ancestor feels peaceful and bright. Then reorient yourself to your own body. You may have to find and heal the corresponding trauma in yourself.

Vortices

Another type of trauma that involves images of ancestors. You might feel yourself spinning, or feel dizzy, or you might visually perceive a tornado somewhere in your body. Put your awareness right in the middle of the spinning, abandoning yourself completely to the movement; sink into that spinning until it stops. You're likely to sense a group of people, often feeling like 'ancient ones', at that point (some people just perceive a collective of vague oval shapes). Merge with the central figure; if there isn't a clear ringleader then merge with the group collectively. Heal whatever sensations you find until the whole group disappears or becomes a cloud of brightness. Occasionally there are two ringleaders to heal.

Past lives

You can tell a past life apart from a generational trauma because the past-life person really feels like you. Past lives are nearly always red herrings. We move into them when our present-life traumas are too threatening. Unless you need the practice, return to the same body sensations and emotions in your present life. The only exception I've seen so far was my death in what appears to be my very most recent past life. Only the very last moment of my death needed healing.

Projections

You really, really think the issue belongs to someone else. You're fine, but the problem is that your partner has power issues, your neighbour is a drama queen, your kids keep lying to you, your boss is evil.

Because merging directly with people who are alive in the present can pose a hazard, I offer a way to merge only with the *qualities* you see in them.

First, make a mental caricature of the person who bothers you. Include all the bothersome aspects. Go wild; lay it on with a spatula. Next, imagine yourself plastering all those annoying characteristics onto a three-dimensional voodoo doll or a generic grey blob or any image that will take it on.

At this point, if the emotions *about* the projection are overwhelming, they must be healed first.

Then merge with this construct, *not with the real person.* Love yourself as the one plastered with all these annoying characteristics. Scan your body for new or exacerbated emotions and body sensations, and heal these in the usual way. Check your work by looking at your perception of the annoying person. If anything still bothers you, repeat the exercise for the remaining aspects.

Dilemmas

You find yourself faced with an impossible choice, either in the present or at a regression moment in the past. You're damned if you do, and damned if you don't. Instead of trying to choose what logically should be the best course of action, sit exactly in the middle. Go to the moment when you're on the cusp of a decision, the moment just before deciding on a course of action. Feel the full force of the dilemma. Stay in this moment and heal the emotions and body sensations. The dilemma will eventually spontaneously resolve, either with one of the choices becoming the obvious right one, or else in ways you would not have foreseen: either by a glorious reframing or with a euphoric third solution that had previously eluded you completely.

Structures in your body

Another rare instance. You see or sense solid objects in your body, like rods connecting points together, or containers enclosing an area. Stay in the sensation until the object dissolves. Feel around the object for any sensation of 'holding on to it' and heal that also. If healing is slow, be sure to include in your sense of self the area just above your forehead, and love yourself as that area too.

Transpersonal experiences and peak states

You might move into some of those after healing certain traumas. Enjoy! The experience should be comfortable, even if it is extremely intense. If there's any fear or discomfort, be sure to heal that. (If the discomfort involves a god-like creature that seems very intimidating, see the section on archetypes and make sure it isn't one of those.) Make a note of the last trauma moment you healed. If the experience or peak state becomes inaccessible again, you might regain it by going back to that moment and healing any remaining traumas.

No time to finish

If you run out of time, quit on a win: stop at the first occasion when a trauma releases and you temporarily feel better. Note how you're feeling and what you've healed so far. By rereading your initial trauma description and these notes, you can re-trigger yourself and finish the healing when you have time. In the meantime, return to the present and love yourself for whatever you're feeling. Then use gratitude to bring yourself all the way into the present: find something—anything—to feel grateful about. Feel that gratitude, both as a feeling and as a body sensation. Promise yourself to return to the unfinished trauma.

Chapter 2

The Prerequisites

This chapter explores the concepts that form the foundation of Whole-Hearted Healing. It introduces the components of the healing technique one by one, with short exercises that will allow you to experience each component from the inside before you try your first solo healing. *The exercises in this chapter are not healing techniques in their own right.* They show ways to broaden your spectrum of perceptions, to access the past more rapidly, and to speed up the release of traumas. The background information shows why and how the technique works. My hope is to remove the mystery from the healing technique — there's enough mystery in the past itself! — and to give you tools for trouble-shooting when the need arises.

In class, we only devote a few minutes to each exercise. There's nothing terribly earth-shaking in here. One exception is Monti Scribner's 'triune brain therapy'. I present it here as a quick exercise in sensing the motivations of different parts of your consciousness, but you may also return to it after you've mastered Whole-Hearted Healing or other power therapies, and use it as a full-fledged healing format.

The Hendricks Loving-Yourself Technique

This seemingly innocuous technique turns out to be a magnificent tool to speed up the release of old traumas. It also helps when old injuries are so deep seated that we can't access them in the first place. Its power occasionally surprises even our most advanced healers. Gay Hendricks, who wrote extensively about body-centred therapy, describes it in his *Loving Yourself Workbook*. Barbara Brennan also gives a one-line description of it in her book *Hands of Light*, in the section on self-care for the healer.

Grant noticed that when we think of loving ourselves, we often reproduce the ways we've been loved in the past, with their attendant strings attached. It's quite common for people to visualise leaning over their child-selves and giving them hugs, for example. There are two problems with this. First, when I'm doing this, am I in my body in the traumatic moment? Probably not. Most likely, I'm being the adult 'me', leaning over and loving, and the one needing love is still dissociated. Oops. And second, while my parents did a stellar job of raising me, I've still managed to associate a certain amount of abandonment and betrayal with motherly and fatherly hugs, or lack of hugs. And while I love my children beyond anything in the world, my own motherly love wasn't necessarily always devoid of extraneous baggage. So I build that into my self-loving too. Now imagine people with *serious* abandonment issues. This kind of self-loving would be downright toxic to them.

What to do, what to do? Hendricks suggests several exercises; one of them is particularly simple and adapts very well to our work. Try it on yourself right now.

Exercise: Loving yourself

Think of something that's really, really easy to love. To avoid mixed feelings, it's best not to use your mate, parents or children. Some people use a more distant relative, a long-time family friend who was always a good fairy to them, or a small child. Animals work well too: a favourite pet, a horse you were allowed to ride. I myself couldn't find any people or animals that fit the bill, so I chose a landscape: a small stream running through a forest. I've seen a few people choose a plant. A rose. An apple tree loaded with fruit.

So: close your eyes, relax for a few moments, and think about this person or animal or thing that's so utterly easy to love. Keep that going until you feel that love flowing nicely.

Now turn some of this love towards yourself. Just deviate some of it, as if you were bending a garden hose back towards yourself, and let it splash all over you. Notice how it feels inside your body. Does the sensation have a temperature, a tactile quality, a colour, a texture? Sit there for a moment, learning how it feels to simply love yourself.

Another, equally effective way to do this: pretend that a picture of this 'something easy to love' is sitting inside your heart. Love it in that location until the feeling is nice and strong. Then let the picture dissolve, while you maintain the feeling of love. [4]

Try both versions of the technique, and decide for yourself which one works best for you.

Exercise: Loving yourself while you feel good

Think about something wonderful. Generate any sort of positive feeling in yourself.

Now love yourself, using the technique you just tried, while feeling wonderful. How does it modify the experience?

Exercise: Loving yourself when you feel awful

Now think about something you really do not want to think about. Stay inside your body and feel what it feels like.

Once you have that, love yourself while having that rotten feeling. Love yourself, not despite that rotten feeling, but *because of it.* This is not about loving the rotten feeling itself, but about loving *yourself* for having landed in that situation.

For example, let's say you feel sad. What is it like to love yourself in this simple, no-strings-attached way, not just despite the sadness, but also *with* the sadness? Because of the sadness? How does it change your experience?

[4] I deliberately use the word 'picture' here. Merging with a person who is alive in the present can be risky, so make sure you just put an *image* of the loveable one in your heart.

Or imagine a situation when your mate says, 'listen, we gotta talk', and the familiar dread kicks in. Now suppose that you sit and listen while loving yourself, exactly as you are, dread, defensiveness and all. How does that change the experience?

Exercise: Coming back to the present: Loving yourself with gratitude

If the previous exercise has kicked you into some traumatic feelings, or anytime you need to come back to an even keel, do the following:

First, love yourself for having this distressing feeling. Boost that love as much as you can. If possible, add any feeling of happiness you can generate to the love *and* the distressing feeling.

Next, orient yourself in the present. Look at your surroundings.

Now think about something you're grateful for. It doesn't have to be anything big. Breath entering your lungs. Warm socks on your feet. Air on your skin. Anything will do. Magnify that feeling of gratitude, as an emotion, as a tactile feeling, as a way of being.

Now give that feeling an extra boost: love yourself while feeling grateful. Hold the gratitude and the self-love together for a few moments. Repeat as needed. This technique works because whenever we're anything but calm, peaceful and light, we in fact are in the past, revisiting some old trauma. Gratitude puts us back into the present. It doesn't matter who or what you're feeling gratitude towards, by the way. Gratitude doesn't necessarily change anything for divinity or the saints or the earth or whomever we decide to be grateful to. Gratitude changes *us.* [5]

---

[5] I strongly recommend the work of Jacquelyn Aldana (*The Fifteen-Minute Miracle*) to anyone who's interested in doing some long-term work on peak states. To my more reserved, northern eyes, her writing is a bit, um, exuberant, but she's done a lot of thinking about how and why gratitude works. Her techniques work so well that she offers a money-back guarantee on her workshops. So overlook the book's tone if you need to; the contents are well worth anyone's time.

Practice loving yourself

Before trying Whole-Hearted Healing, I suggest you practise this loving-yourself technique for a day or so. You'll need to juggle it with other things while healing, so it'll be easier if you can call it up easily.

Practise loving yourself when you feel good. But more importantly, practise it while you feel bad. Practise it in all sorts of settings. This will lay the groundwork for Whole-Hearted Healing.

"But I get all sorts of fear when I try this"

I've had a few clients for whom this technique felt very threatening. I'll discuss this more at length in the next chapter. For the moment, don't sweat it; there are ways to heal with a slightly different feeling, such as 'accepting and honouring yourself' instead of 'loving yourself'. Also, do use the 'gratitude' exercise, even if you can't add self-love to it; it works very well on its own. I do suggest you heal your discomfort with loving yourself as soon as possible, especially if you're planning to use WHH long term. There's a step-by-step method for doing this in appendix A. The last example in Chapter 3 includes a transcript from such a session.

The Centre of Awareness: an Experiential Definition of the Self

There are many confusing and overlapping ways to define 'the self'. We use a simple, experiential definition, leaving aside philosophical considerations. We locate the area in our bodies that feels like "us" and dub this our Centre of Awareness (CoA for short).

This is an interesting concept to play with if we want to reclaim the parts of our psyches that have gone underground. Most people find that they can move their CoA around to different parts of their body. By doing so, we can, in effect, tune in to forgotten or neglected parts of ourselves.

Tracking our CoA is also revealing of our long-term progress in healing: most people who use Whole-Hearted Healing and other power therapies long term find that their CoA changes location and size over time.

Exercise: Finding your Centre of Awareness[6]

Close your eyes. Get a sense of where "you" are in your body. It helps to point your finger at yourself, keeping your finger an inch or two away from your skin, starting at your forehead and working your way down your midline. There's a slight pull of recognition at the point where "you" are. Keep scanning all the way down your body. Are "you" in a pinpoint location, or more diffusely spread over a larger area? Some people have more than one Centre of Awareness. If you do, which one has the strongest pull of recognition?

Sometimes the results teach us something new about ourselves. One memorable week, I had two clients in a row start this exercise by saying, "That's easy. I live in my heart!" I had them do the scan anyway, "just to check." "Oops! There it is! Right up in my forehead!"

Exercise: Moving your Centre of Awareness

Close your eyes. Feel your CoA as it is.

Now go exploring. Move your CoA to different parts of your body. Just relax and imagine that 'you' are your heart. It may help to touch your heart area — I find that a very light touch with one or two fingers works best. Wait a minute or two, just hanging out. Sometimes it takes that long to get any sensations. How does life feel from the centre of your chest?

Now continue your explorations: How does it feel to be your lower belly? How about your hands? Your forehead (if your CoA wasn't there in the first place)? Your feet?

This isn't an earth-shaking exercise. The changes in cognition are subtle, in most cases. If some distressing feelings or sensations arise, stay with the sensations, and use the Loving-Yourself technique, loving yourself *from* that area of your body, just being there and loving yourself with no agenda to change. Maintain this for a few moments, then take a

[6] Adapted from the *Basic Whole-Hearted Healing™ Manual.*

gentle, deep breath and return to the present. Use the Gratitude exercise to bring yourself into the here-and-now.

"But I can't move my CoA at all"

Some people's Centre of Awareness is locked in one place. If this seems to be your case, try a slightly different approach: *focus your attention* on the different areas of your body instead. It's not quite the same as feeling from *inside*, but it will work well enough to allow you to sense and release traumas.

If you can move your awareness to some areas of your body and not to others, use the same stopgap method for the troublesome areas.

Here, from Grant and Tal, are a few more ideas to try if you find it difficult to move your CoA. They all achieve the same result; sometimes it's simply a matter of finding the right metaphor for what we're trying to do.

> Tal: "See an image of yourself, in front of you, as if you were a statue or a doll (yes, the image can be animate), and enter the body you see before you in the place you want your COA to be."
>
> Grant: "Another cute trick is to physically move the body area *to* the stuck CoA. Although sometimes the acrobatics are just impossible..."
>
> Tal: "A few more tricks:
>
> - "Place your hand on your present (stuck) COA location; then move the hand slowly across your body, keeping your COA under it. If you encounter difficulty, use EFT or WHH to release the resistance, (you'll be able to do this later on) and continue until your COA is in the desired location.
> - "If your CoA is stuck in your head, imagine your physical brain, grey matter and all, moving slowly around your body, processing information from each location that it is in.
> - "Imagine that you are "sitting" in the location in your body where you wish your COA to be."

After you have become used to Whole-Hearted Healing, go to appendix B for a step-by-step method to regain access to your whole body.

The Triune Brain: Redefining the Subconscious

(Adapted from *Peak States of Consciousness Vol. 1,* by Grant McFetridge)

Dr. MacLean's three-part model of the human brain

A very neglected breakthrough in understanding brain biology forms the basis of a three-part or 'triune' model of the brain. In the 1960s, Dr. Paul MacLean, at the National Institute for Mental Health, expanding on the work of James Papez, described a three-part concentric layering structure to the human brain. The outermost layer is the neomammalian brain, the neocortex, which is the seat of thought and most voluntary movement. The next layer inward is the paleomammalian brain, composed of the limbic system, which is the seat of our emotions and autonomic nervous system. In the innermost portion sits the reptilian brain, composed of the brain stem, midbrain, basal ganglia and other structures. Each brain serves different functions (with some overlap), but Dr. MacLean postulated that the integration, or coordination, between the brains is inadequate, and that this inadequate integration is a genetic problem in our species.

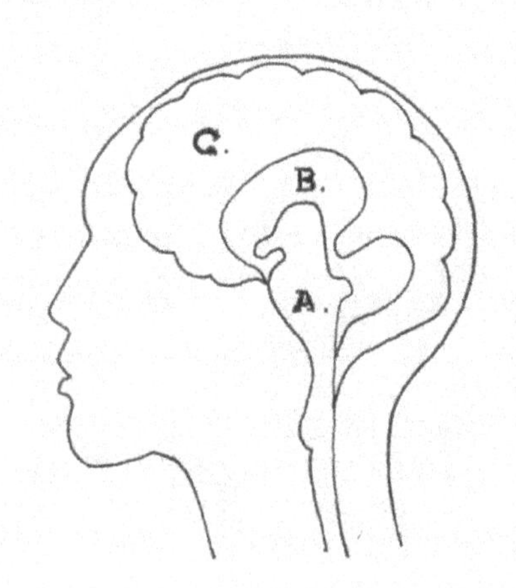

Figure 1: A simplified view of the triune brains: A. the body brain, better known as the reptilian brain, corresponds to the brain stem. B. the heart brain, or paleomammalian brain, corresponds to the limbic system; and C. the mind brain, or neomammalian brain, corresponds to the neocortex.

Triune brain structure and inner experience

How does the triune structure of the brain apply to our inner experience? In everyday terms, we know these brains as the 'mind', 'heart', and 'body'. Each brain has different biological functions and abilities. The 'mind', or neocortex, is the part of ourselves we most often think of as who we are. It perceives itself as being in the head, and it is the part of ourselves that forms judgments, handles short-term memory, and does abstractions like mathematics. One of its primary functions is handling and manipulating audible sounds and language. The 'heart' is the limbic system in the brain, yet perceives itself as being in the chest, probably because this is the area of its primary biological responsibility and sensory awareness. It allows us to feel emotions, and to be emotionally aware (either positively or negatively) of the presence of others. One of its primary functions is handling visual imagery. Finally, the 'body' consciousness (or *hara* in Japanese) is composed of the tissues at the base of our skull, and probably other distributed systems in our body. It experiences itself in the lower belly, its area of major biological function. This brain gives us a sense of time and our ability to feel sexuality. We communicate with this brain when we do dowsing or muscle testing. One of its primary functions is handling physical sensations, and probably scent as well.

Independent self-awareness in each brain

The most difficult conceptual jump you must make to understand Dr. MacLean's work is to realize that each of the brains is intelligently, independently self-aware. Because we tend to assume that thinking requires words, it's difficult for us to realize that the heart and body brains actually think. In fact, only the mind thinks in words; the heart thinks in sequences of feelings, and the body thinks in gestalt sequences of body sensations (described as the 'felt sense' in Eugene Gendlin's *Focusing*). By this, I don't mean that it's as if there were three people inside of us. Instead, since each brain is so different, we might compare this situation to that of a living stereo system. Imagine if the speakers (mind), tape deck (heart), and receiver (body) were each self-aware, each trying to run the show and each puzzled because the other parts won't do what it wants them to. It would be hard to imagine how a stereo like this would ever manage to play music! And unfortunately, this is fairly close to the mark. Although they share much sensory data and awareness of each other's actions, each brain tends to be in denial about the existence of the others. In fact, the brains often come into conflict, even to the point of overtly or unconsciously attempting to manipulate and control each other. A simple illustration of this is when you're sexually attracted (the body consciousness) to someone you don't even like (the emotional consciousness), and are confused about the situation (the mind consciousness).

In most people, the brains interact like members of a dysfunctional family. Generally, one of the brains ends up dominating the others. People tend to lead their lives and act in ways that reflect this dominance. We've all seen extreme examples of people who are driven by their feelings, or totally oriented towards satisfying body sensations, or completely analytical, although the pattern is present to some degree in most people. (...)

Trauma and the triune brain model

The final element of the basic model involves the phenomenon of trauma. For almost everyone, remembered or forgotten traumas drive most of our behavior and emotional life, completely outside of our conscious awareness. Traumatic experiences are stored, and later 'played back' as outer circumstances trigger us. This playback is an entire bodily experience, as if our younger traumatized self is partially taking over our body. (...) From a biological viewpoint, storing and automatically using our responses to traumatic experiences makes sense, since we survived the experience by responding in those ways. Unfortunately, what may have been a good evolutionary strategy for our animal ancestors is a tragic problem in our complex sapient lives. (...)

This simple model of the psyche is compatible with Western cultural biases and explains many psychological phenomena. For another viewpoint on trauma and the triune brain biological model, I refer you to Dr. Janov's *The Anatomy of Mental Illness* or *The New Primal Scream.*

Body consciousness associations and the Developmental Events Model

(...) Because the body brain is often referred to as the reptilian brain, people often get the impression that it is slow and stupid. The truth is just the opposite; it is not only self-aware, it is probably the smartest of the brains. However, it is severely limited by its biologically-dictated thinking processes. Indeed, this kind of thinking causes severe and tragic problems for humanity, as well as for other species. As noted above, the body consciousness thinks in sequences of body sensations. Extending this concept, when the body learns, it does so by 'associating' two or more sensations together. It does *not* use judgment like our mind brain does. In evolutionary terms, the ability to form judgments came much later, after the mind brain evolved. These body brain associations that have no element of judgment are the cause of most of the problems in our lives, particularly the severe or life-threatening problems. In an extreme example, early *in utero* associations can be so inflexible that if they involve survival issues the person will actually die trying to follow through with what his body feels he has to do to survive. Addictions are generally due to this type of problem (although they can have other causes): the body is convinced, from early association, that it needs the addicting substance to survive, and it is unable to acknowledge the fact that the substance is slowly killing it, along with ruining the person's life.

Example:

It was years before I realized I was sexually attracted to angry women. I had mistakenly thought I was attracted to them in spite of their anger. The reason turned out to be a series of *in utero* traumas. In them, I was being physically hurt and struggling to survive while my mom was feeling angry. My body consciousness had associated my survival with being surrounded by the emotion of anger. These women had exactly the same tone of anger as my mom had had. In fact, if they ever stopped being angry, I would unconsciously stimulate them again into anger, because to my body consciousness it felt like I might die if that emotion wasn't nearby. My body used the mechanism of sexual attraction to make me behave in ways it desired. (...)

Additional brain structures

The triune brain model fits our personal experiences of the mind, heart and body quite well. It also is quite useful in explaining a lot of the different kinds of material that we as therapists and healers encounter in our work. However, as my colleagues and I became more experienced, we found there were some brain interactions that we didn't understand. Eventually, we realized that although there were three primary brains, there existed two more 'sub-brains'—the solar plexus brain and the crown brain—for a total of five distinct brain structures in post-birth human beings. And our observations turned out to reflect underlying brain biology: Dr. MacLean, in his text on the triune brain, identifies five separate brain structures forming on the early zygote's spinal cord.

The Solar Plexus Brain

The most important of these sub-brains experiences itself normally at the solar plexus, and so for simplicity we call it the 'solar plexus brain'. Like the other triune brains, it also has its own self-awareness. Its role seems to be about power: from the amount of physical energy we have, to psychological and spiritual issues of personal power.

Normally, this brain is merged and somewhat indistinguishable from the body consciousness.

The Crown Brain

The other sub-brain is one we call the 'crown brain', because of its experiential location. Although it usually is merged with the mind brain, and hence indistinguishable, when it is split away it experiences itself centered above the physical head. When it is separate, it can feel like a massive Buddhist statue floating over one's head. One of the main functions of this brain is to interact with the 'outside' world, most obviously its spiritual aspects.

The Placental and Sperm Tail Brains

Another two brains exist but since they die off *in utero*, we don't normally refer to them in our normal post-birth description of the triune brain system. However, to our great surprise they are critical to a very important peak state called Wholeness, and are also very important to *in utero* trauma.

The first of these is the organelle 'brain' which is in the tail portion of the sperm, and dies off during conception. For simplicity, we call it the 'sperm tail brain'. [*Since publication of* Peak States of Consciousness, Vol. 1, *we've taken to calling this wee chunk of awareness the* spine brain, *to better reflect its role in the post-birth body.]*

The second 'brain' is in an organelle structure in the egg, which later develops into the placenta and dies during birth. Again for simplicity we call it the 'placental brain'. (Note that the placenta is part of the baby, not part of the mother.)

For a long time we thought these structures simply died off when their physical roles ended, but report after report from people completing the healing of those events shows that the 'essence' of both the placenta and the sperm tail becomes integrated in our bodies. The adult 'placental brain' has a role in protecting us from disease, and the 'sperm tail brain' helps support the other brains, integrating the brains (unless trauma blocks this) and also integrating the physical and transpersonal aspects of our lives. [7]

An update...

As if this wasn't enough bits of consciousness to worry about, our work since the publication of the above excerpt shows *two more* self-

[7] In *The New Primal Scream*, Janov repeatedly refers to 'the mind of the immune system'. This is almost certainly what we call the placental brain.

aware brains: one at the perineum, associated with the egg, and one at the third eye, associated with the sperm. They can be extremely difficult to perceive because they usually merge with the body brain. The third eye, true to many spiritual traditions, seems to have a role in clairvoyance. The perineal (or 'Base') brain appears to have a role in sexuality and reproduction, plus a support role in clairvoyant seeing.

In his recent classes, Grant has taken to calling the Buddha brain "crown brain", which does make more sense. It is always at the crown, but it is not necessarily experienced as a huge Buddha! I will shamelessly flip-flop between the two names in this text.

Redefining the subconscious

The basic part of the triune brain theory, after mouldering in obscurity for many years, has recently hit the mainstream. Several volumes on the different types of learning related to each brain, and on the emotional ramifications of the model, now populate library shelves. I particularly recommend *A General Theory of Love*, by Drs. Thomas Lewis, Fari Amini and Richard Lannon.

The wilder parts of the theory ('*sperm tail brain*'???) are much harder to accept. But in fact, belief is completely beside the point. We can take this as literal truth or, if that's too strange, we can simply use it as a model, a system for accessing all the hidden parts of us, the parts that we used to call the subconscious. We use the model experientially, and it works.

This model is important because it allows us to quit considering the subconscious as this vague black hole whose dark aspects might jump out at any moment to wreck our lives. The subconscious isn't *out there*, it's right in here and, once we learn to use the tools, fully accessible. One could even re-label it as the 'not-yet-conscious', but I'll stick with tradition for the sake of tolerable writing.

What happens when we work from the model of a consciousness that tends to partition itself when traumatized?

- We can assume that these variously integrated self-aware bits are *us*. As an example, consider a client who is struggling to lose weight and wails, "My body keeps betraying me!" Well, guess what. His body doesn't live in the next town over.

- We can understand, and therefore become compassionate about, our very human tendency to project the less-loveable parts of ourselves on other people or on anything else that's handy. We can reintegrate and heal these lost aspects of us.

- We can assume that most of the extensive menagerie of spirits, angels, demons, archetypes and sub-deities that people encounter in regression, breathwork, dreams, or when taking hallucinogens are in fact more projections of unhealed parts of *us*.

- We can reintegrate all those bit-players, and, when we do, we end up with a simplified universe where we are active participants, not helpless puppets.

- The transpersonal experiences and peak states that remain after this cleanup intersect nicely with mystical traditions from all parts of the world, and with the implications of the more far-out theories of contemporary physics.

"*Take your life in your own hands, and what happens? A terrible thing: no one to blame.*" — Erica Jong[8]

Working with the Brains

By Monti Scribner
(Used and adapted by kind permission)

Imagine that you are living in your very own personal soap opera - it might not be so hard to do!

In your soap opera, you (the main character) are always clueless about things that are obvious to the viewing audience. Thus, you make decisions based upon your perceived reality, while other characters (your brains) attempt to sabotage your goals because they have their own agendas. It helps if you imagine that you are living with a crew of independently self-aware friends who are very invested in the outcome of each of your decisions, and each has their own (sometimes peculiar) agenda.

[8] Quoted in Julia Cameron, *The Artist's Way*, P. 74

As described in *Peak States of Consciousness Vol. 1 and Vol. 2*, each of the brains has its own compelling agenda, with the Body brain being dominant. So far we know that their locations and general agendas are:

1) **Buddha Brain**, also known as **Crown Brain**—top of the head—connects us with the 'outside', especially the spiritual or transpersonal aspects of life.
2) **Third Eye** -- middle of the forehead -- clairvoyance; and
3) **Mind Brain**—in the head—understanding. Forms judgments, handles short-term memory and abstractions, handles and manipulates audible sounds and language.
4) **Sperm Tail Brain**, also known as **Spine Brain**—middle of the upper back—support and integration.
5) **Heart Brain**—in the center of the chest—connecting. Thinks in sequences of emotions.
6) **Solar Plexus brain**—in the solar plexus—energy, personal power and connection to the universe.
7) **Placental Brain**—in the navel—protection.
8) **Body Brain**—in the lower belly—survival. Thinks in gestalt sequences of body sensations and has no concept of the future.
9) **Perineal** or **Base Brain** -- at perineum -- sexuality, reproduction and clairvoyance.

Your brains can sabotage your ability to solve your personal problems because, based upon past perceived traumas, they developed distorted perceptions. This is where the soap opera kicks in.

To identify the brains' perceptions and agendas, it helps if you release any judgment or preconceived ideas while you extrapolate their possible viewpoints about a problem into dramatic scenarios.

Try to have some fun with it; the brains' perceptions don't have to make logical sense.

Exercise: Triune Brain Therapy

First, think about the emotion/pain/problem you are experiencing. Then, place your awareness into each brain in turn (just as you did in the last exercise, *Moving your CoA*) and see whether you can sense which one is reacting with resistance or emotion. If a brain feels soft and neutral and you sense a feeling of calm, peace, love or happiness, that brain is not resisting or reacting to the problem.

If you sense that a brain is reacting with resistance or an emotional "charge," keep your centre of awareness in the brain, and then *imagine that this particular brain expands to become as large as you are, and your entire body is the brain.* At the same time, try to get a sense of the personality of this brain by being aware of its point of view (example: the Heart brain will communicate with emotions).

If you are new to Whole-Hearted Healing and other power therapies, end the exercise here, after scanning each brain and learning more about its reactions. Use gratitude (see p. 36) to bring yourself back to the present. You can come back to this exercise anytime after you get comfortable with healing yourself, and complete it by healing any resistance from your personal tribe of brains.

If you are already familiar with EFT, TAT or other rapid healing techniques, use these now to eliminate the emotional resistance from each brain.

When you think there is no charge left, you can dig deeper by identifying associated (soap opera) possibilities and see how you, and the brains, react.

Here are a few examples (note that, for the sake of simplicity, the placenta, spine, perineum and third eye are not included in this work):

1) You want to increase your confidence and sense of personal power. When you think about your goal and imagine soap-opera explanations for the brains' possible agendas, you get a "charge" on the following: the Buddha brain believes that it will die if it becomes too powerful. The Mind brain may not understand what it means to be powerful. The Heart brain is afraid to be assertive because it believes it must please everyone. The Body brain wants to delay the work necessary to become assertive by distracting you. The Solar Plexus brain asks, "Why do I think I can be better than anyone else"?

2) Your friend asks you for a ride to the gas station and you agree to take her, although a part of you feels resentful and unhappy. You move your CoA into your Mind brain, begin doing EFT on the resistance, and determine that your Mind brain is thinking "gas is expensive and I know she won't offer to pay me for the ride." You then move your CoA to your Heart brain, which is thinking "she only wants to use me and she has never done anything nice for me!" Your Solar Plexus brain is thinking "If I take her, she will think I'll do other things for her." As a result of these conflicting messages, you may take your friend to the gas station, but you won't feel very good about it until you heal the brains' agendas.

3) You are experiencing physical pain, and want to determine whether your brains are resisting your ability to heal. When you connect with the

Buddha brain, you determine that it doesn't want to let go of the pain because the pain gives you a reason to take care of yourself. The Heart brain likes holding on to the emotions associated with the pain and is afraid that it won't know itself without the pain; the Body brain thinks that if it keeps everything the same, it will feel safe.

In summary:

- Familiarize yourself with the brains' agendas;
- Think about the issue you want to resolve, and how you feel about it;
- Place your CoA into one brain at a time, and sense whether it is resisting or has an emotional "charge" associated with the issue. (You can begin to use power therapies at this point); and
- Dig deeper by imagining what each brain might be thinking which could sabotage your ability to resolve your problem.
- If you are already familiar with some power therapies, continue to do EFT or similar healing techniques until the resistance or emotional "charge" is completely gone. (Again, if you're new at this, just use the exercise to explore, and then use gratitude to bring yourself back into the present.)

Monti Scribner
5/14/05

COEX Systems or Trauma stacks: a Shortcut to the Past

You may have noticed that we all have series of traumas that share a common theme. It's as if we kept rehearsing the same types of problems, over and over. We choose series of partners who present us with the same conflicts, or we repeatedly get one type of physical injury. A friend of mine was involved in three accidental minor fires in a row. Then there's one of my relatives who owns a restaurant. Last year, just as the busy season kicked in, her automatic dishwasher broke down. Three days later, her big cook stove packed it in. The next week her dishwasher broke down again. Five days later it was the freezer's turn, then dishwasher, Part Three. While she drove to town to pick up the repaired dishwasher after Episode Three, her car broke down. [9]

We all could come up with examples of that kind of pattern. At a deeper level, it's even more evident. We find ourselves having, for example, a series of problems about abandonment, showing up first with

[9] I can't resist passing on the comment Grant wrote on my manuscript: "I knew this guy who broke his leg sixteen times by the age of nineteen!"

our parents then with our mates and coworkers and then with the therapist we seek help from, and even in brief vignettes with strangers.

Dr. Stanislav Grof, a pioneer in the study of human consciousness, first coined the term *COEX system*, short for 'system of condensed experience', for those thematic trauma series.

> A COEX *system* can be defined as a specific constellation of memories consisting of condensed experiences (and related fantasies) from different life periods of the individual. The memories belonging to a particular COEX system have a similar basic theme or contain similar elements and are associated with a strong charge of the same quality. (...) Each COEX system has a basic theme that permeates all its layers and represents their common denominator; the nature of these themes varies considerably from one COEX constellation to another. Various layers of a particular system can, for example, contain all memories of the past exposures to humiliating and degrading situations that have damaged [a person's] self-esteem. In other instances, the common element can be anxiety experienced in regard to shocking and frightening events, claustrophobic and suffocating feelings evoked by various oppressive and restricting circumstances where there was no possibility of fighting back and defending oneself or escaping, as well as an intense sense of guilt and moral failure triggered by a number of specific situations.[10]

I would modify Dr. Grof's definition in two ways. First, I tend to think of COEX systems as *strings of traumas* rather than *constellations.* Although they sometimes form complex systems, traumas with similar themes tend to be arranged in a linear way rather than in loose clusters. People with advanced healing abilities can actually see those thematic traumas as a series of frozen 'shapes' or frozen moments in time, joined by a sort of string: a visual timeline. Second, Dr. Grof considers most COEX systems to originate at or around our birth. Over fifteen years of regression and experimentation, our Institute members and their clients have consistently observed that the origin of COEX systems is almost always prenatal, and that prenatal consciousness begins much, much earlier than birth.

Although this may look depressing at first sight, from a healing point of view, the existence of COEX systems is excellent news. After he'd spent a frustrating and laborious few months healing each and every instance of trauma one by one, Grant discovered that these connected strings of

---

[10] Stanislav Grof, *Realms of the Human Unconscious*, 1975, pp. 46-47.

traumas *do not have to be healed individually.* Going to the earliest one in the series is enough. Once we completely heal the source of a pattern, the whole trauma stack resolves. It means, for example, that survivors of physical abuse do not necessarily have to relive every single occurrence in all its details. They must simply identify the theme (a certain emotional tone, a certain sort of physical sensation, a certain core belief), follow the pattern to the earliest recalled event, and use that as a starting point for regression. As we gain experience in regression, we become able to access the very early prenatal events with increasing ease, and move more and more directly to the origin of each pattern.

Sometimes, during a healing session, we get flooded with multiple memories. A swarm of events surfaces; confusion threatens. The existence of COEXes dictates an easy solution: always attend to the earliest event. The later ones will resolve spontaneously, or else they'll lose most of their charge and be easy to clean up later in the session.

Exercise: The mote in thy neighbour's eye

It's always easier to see patterns in other people, so let's start there. Think of a trauma magnet or drama king or queen that you know. Sketch out a COEX string of one of his or her drama themes. Draw a series of connecting shapes like the ones in *Figure 2* on page 52. Start at the top, closest to the present; each box represents one event in a string of related problems. Be as ungenerous and judgemental as you like, invent wildly if you must. Try to imagine what kinds of childhood traumas would have set the pattern up. Then — why not? — imagine what similarly-patterned events could have happened before birth.

Last, identify the string's connecting theme and write it as a title.

I've picked my good friend Cinderella.
(I hear she's been doing much better lately.)

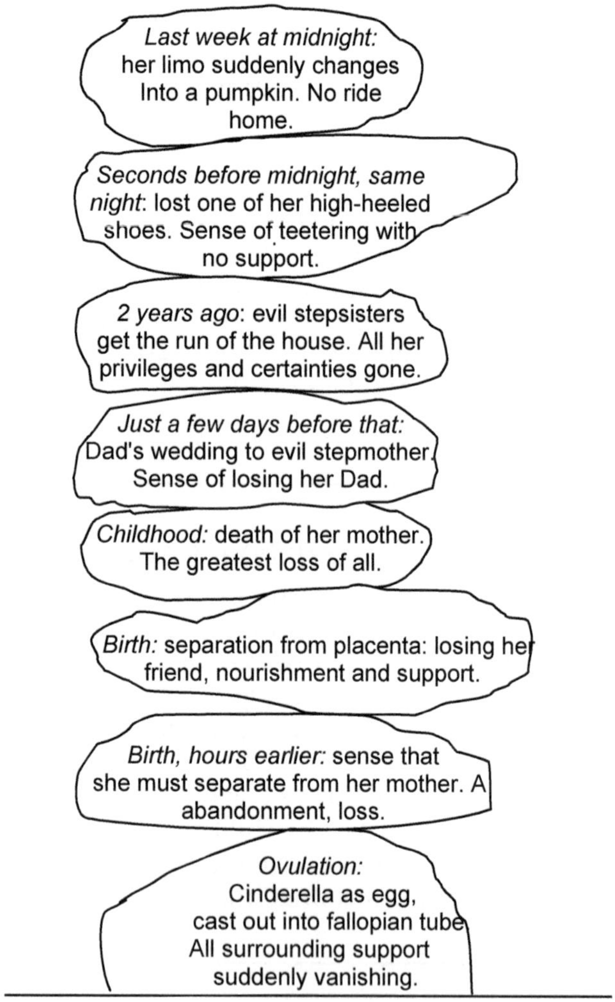

Last week at midnight: her limo suddenly changes Into a pumpkin. No ride home.

Seconds before midnight, same night: lost one of her high-heeled shoes. Sense of teetering with no support.

2 years ago: evil stepsisters get the run of the house. All her privileges and certainties gone.

Just a few days before that: Dad's wedding to evil stepmother. Sense of losing her Dad.

Childhood: death of her mother. The greatest loss of all.

Birth: separation from placenta: losing her friend, nourishment and support.

Birth, hours earlier: sense that she must separate from her mother. A abandonment, loss.

Ovulation: Cinderella as egg, cast out into fallopian tube All surrounding support suddenly vanishing.

Common theme: Abandonment, loss of support, loss of everything taken for granted.

Figure 2: The mote in thy neighbour's eye.

Exercise: The beam in your own eye

Now do the same exercise, but with yourself as the subject. The theme does not have to be the same as in the exercise above, of course. Just pick a string of incidents that have a common theme or flavour. If you don't remember the childhood events connected to it, take some wild guesses. Feeling brave? Reconstruct what might have happened *in utero*, based on what you know about your mother's gestation and the circumstances of your birth. Just imagine it. (See *Figure 3*.)

If the exercise brought up some discomfort from the traumas you tracked down, take a moment to sit with it. Do not avoid the emotions and body sensations; just be in your body and love yourself, using the technique you learned at the beginning of this chapter. Just love yourself exactly as you are, with no agenda to change anything. Note any changes that happen. Then, after a few minutes, use gratitude to bring yourself back to the present.

Here's one of mine:

Recently: looking at current events, sudden fear of major disaster and penury. Impulse to hoard stuff.

29 years old: single mother with 3 kids. Changes in the income assistance system threaten to leave me without enough money to pay the rent. Unsubstantiated fear but feel awful for 2 weeks.

28 years old: marital break-up. Homeless for a short period. Fear of upcoming winter.

19 years old: choose partner and lifestyle that will keep me a pauper. Pattern lasts about 6 years.

Childhood: games about storing food, making reserves for winter.

Photo of me as a 4-year-old: I'm so tiny, I look as if I belong to another family.

In womb: mother over-tired, maybe anemic. Fetus feels deprived of nutrients.

My mother in womb: Grandmother, already mother of 8, exhausted and maybe anemic.

Common theme: Fear of deprivation.

Figure 3: The beam in your own eye.

Chapter 3

Basic Whole-Hearted Healing

Here we are at last: the main course of this book. If you've never tried Whole-Hearted Healing, please read this chapter in its entirety before starting. Feeling nervous? If you did the previous exercises, you've already used all the components of WHH. Now we're just putting them together.

The Setting

This is an eminently portable technique. You don't need a therapist. You don't need any equipment although I do recommend a notebook. (More about this in a minute.) You only need a bit of privacy, somewhere to sit comfortably or lie down, a chunk of time and the willingness to explore the hidden parts of yourself.

A chunk of time: give yourself at least an hour and a half to two hours for the first few sessions. It's better to have the flexibility to stay longer, although there are ways to work around that. As your skill grows, you'll find two things: one, you'll heal faster; two, you'll learn how to keep the traumas from intruding into the present. Then you'll be able to use shorter sessions productively and without too much discomfort from unfinished issues. Your proficiency may even open the door to the possibility of using very short intervals of time (the five- or ten-minute bits of down-time peppered through our days) to heal issues, one aspect at a time.

What Will We Do, Exactly?

Whole-Hearted Healing is a regression therapy. All we do is use intention or autosuggestion to go inward, sense our feelings and body sensations, and stay with these until something shifts. There are, however, two crucial differences from other regression therapies.

The first difference is what I consider one of Grant's most important discoveries (though he downplays this): to heal a past trauma completely, you must stay in your body, in the past.[11]

I'd like to frame that one, to paint it in the sky:

To heal a trauma completely with this type of technique, you must stay inside your body in the past.

Consider this:

> You remember a traumatic childhood scene. You're five years old... There you are, over there, sitting on the stairs of your grandmother's house, weeping....

Hold it!

Can you see it? You're outside your body. Your five-year-old self isn't *here*, he's *over there*, on the stairs. You can revisit this event time and again, talk to your child-self, tell him it's all okay and you love him, and little will change. Yes, you'll gain a wonderful intellectual understanding of what happened that day, but you will still be compelled to re-enact the pattern that this trauma set in motion. You will still be dissociated, and this very dissociation is what made this event a trauma in the first place.

---

[11] Therapist Ron Mied, working with Grant in the early years, first taught him about the importance of staying inside one's body while working on traumas -- this was one of Ron's key discoveries. During the same period, Grant learned regression through Breathwork from Sheelo Bohm. The conceptual jump was to synthesize elements from both approaches, and apply the concept of staying in-body to prenatal and 'projected' images as well.

When we are under attack, when life becomes temporarily untenable, we flee. This is normal human behaviour. It is protective behaviour. We blank out or dissociate or 'pop out of our bodies' until the coast is clear. By doing so we feel safer, but unfortunately, our deeper nature is to want to experience, to experience *everything.* So we store the experience until it's safe to relive it, or more exactly to *live it fully* for the first time. As long as we haven't fully lived it, the frozen moment—or rather its emotional furniture—returns periodically to wreak havoc in our lives, a reminder: *Haven't I left something unfinished?*

Here's Stanislav Grof again, clearly explaining the concept of dissociation, though as I far as I know he never did make the conceptual jump to its resolution: reliving an event while consciously staying inside one's body.

> It is very likely that in [major trauma] situations of this kind, the original traumatic event was not really fully experienced at the time when it was happening. A massive psychological shock can lead in certain persons to loss of consciousness and swooning. It is conceivable that somewhat less dramatic circumstances can lead to a situation where the experience is shut out partially rather than completely. As a result of this, the event cannot be psychologically 'digested' and integrated, and remains in the psyche as a dissociated foreign element. When it then emerges from the unconscious during psychedelic or holotropic therapy, it is not as much reliving of what happened as it is *the first full experiencing of this event, which makes it possible to complete it and integrate it.* [12]

To resolve a trauma, then, to heal it all the way, we must be in our body. We must relive the event as we failed to live it back then: from the perspective of the inside of our body. It is safe, now. We can feel it happen, love ourselves, and be non-critical as we relive it... until something changes.

And this is the second difference from other regression therapies that I've seen out there: we continue healing until things change quite drastically.

Often the latter part of my first session with a new student will start with the following theme:

> Student: "Okay... I'm now feeling reconciled to the idea that this is happening to me... I'm willing to live with the (*Fill the blank: neglect,*

[12] Stanislav Grof, *The Adventure of Self-Discovery*, p. 225. The emphasis is mine.

abandonment, sadness...)" (*Student starts the motions of coming back to the present)*

Me: "Great! Stay in the past. You're about two thirds of the way there."

This often provokes bewilderment. People who have done talk therapy and various kinds of counselling find it hard to believe that reframing and rationalisation aren't the end of the healing road.

If you're inside your body and you stay in the past beyond this point, larger shifts start to happen.

First, as one event gets fully accessed, you're likely to spontaneously move to earlier and earlier versions of it (this probably started happening before that 'acceptance' moment). Then, you're likely to rerun some slightly improved versions of the event. You stay in the past, maybe moving even earlier, and eventually a big reframing spontaneously occurs. The traumatic theme transforms into a barely-recognizable, positive version of itself. People commonly feel or see a lot of light. There's a completely new perspective.

We stay in the traumatic sensations, moving earlier and earlier in time, until the only feelings left are calm, peace and a light, weightless sensation.

So that's the short version of what we do: we sit quietly, feel into the past, stay in our bodies, love ourselves while reliving the traumatic theme in its various past manifestations, and continue healing long enough: until everything feels calm, peaceful and light.

The Steps

Now let's look in more detail at the steps you saw in Chapter 1.

Step 1: **Find something that's bothering you in the present. Get yourself worked up about it. Write down a few words about how you feel, and about what makes you feel that way.**

Something that's bothering you in the present: anything. Whole-Hearted Healing works best for emotional problems, but like many power therapies, it also works for a number of physical issues, especially if you can access their emotional underpinnings. A surprising number of physical issues are actually held in by emotions. Of course, you won't heal a broken arm, but at minimum you'll be a calm and peaceful person with a broken arm, which is a definite improvement. Plus you might stop in its tracks a pattern or repeated arm injuries or repeated collisions.

So think about something that's bothersome, sink into it: this isn't time for rationalization. Get worked up about it. Go ahead and feel sorry for yourself, just this once.

Write it down. We're back to the notebook issue.

Write it down because it's likely to help you get into the issue. Just a few key words, a sentence or two. How much is it bothering you? Rate it on a scale of zero to ten. Zero is calm, peace and light, ten is the most pain you can imagine. Write it down because it will also help you get more of your consciousness into it. Remember our multiple brains? Putting the problem into words gets your mind-brain into it. But there's more.

As you work your way through the trauma, you can gauge your progress by glancing at your initial notes. If the issue is unfinished, the rereading will trigger you afresh, bringing up different aspects of the problem. And when you're done, you'll know for sure that you're done because the rereading will prompt a reaction like, "Did I really write this?" When you heal an issue completely, its pain rating will be zero out of ten. It'll be so gone that you'll wonder how you could possibly have thought it a problem in the first place. You won't lose memory of the event; but it'll suddenly regain its rightful proportion as one tiny event in a lifetime of events. You'll be ready to move on to the next thing.

And that's the most important reason why you need to write it down: you'll be so ready to move on to the next thing that, without your initial notes, you're likely to forget how much healing you've actually done. Institute members see this in their clients all the time. "My sister's divorce? Oh, that wasn't ever so much of a problem. My *real* problem is that I'm unsatisfied with my job. If you could heal *that*, I'd really believe that this healing method works."[13]

There's one more reason to write down your initial complaint, followed later by session notes: this field is still very new. We're doing a lot of research and finding new applications of WHH and its more

---

[13] This problem is so prevalent with the new 'power' therapies that Roger Callahan, the inventor of Thought Field Therapy (TFT), coined a name for it: it's called the Apex effect. Contrary to traditional talk therapies, power therapies (WHH is one of them) heal traumas so thoroughly that people often forget that they had a problem in the first place.

advanced offshoots every day. If anything very unusual happens, we'd like to hear about it. And it's amazing how quickly one can forget the contents of a healing session. A healing notebook is also a safeguard: if you become seriously stuck, you can trace the problem back and troubleshoot it with a WHH practitioner.

My own notebooks—I'm approaching the end of volume 27 as of this writing—have become the chronicle of a fascinating voyage through consciousness. They're festooned with little tabs made of masking tape, which mark the interesting sightings along the way. Some of those sightings led to major discoveries. Some heralded my entry into wonderful new states of being. My books are journals, safe territories, research tools, platforms for new ideas, private audience for rants that lead to yet more healings. Yeah, I'm a notebook girl through and through.

"But I have a lot of trouble with the written word"

Okay. I've had clients with severe dyslexia. One client with a head injury, limited reading ability, writing skills gone. Fair enough.

First: this isn't a novel or anything for anyone's scrutiny but your own. A few key words are enough. Not everybody's a notebook girl. A few jottings on a chunk of paper will do the job just fine (and you can experiment with healing your discomfort with writing). If this is uncomfortable or impossible, try any of these:

- Enlist a trusted accomplice as a secretary, witness, supporter and guide. Whenever you need to refocus or check your results, ask this wonderful person to read your initial comments back to you. He or she can also keep session notes detailing your progress.

- Use a voice recorder. Play back your initial rant as needed. Add comments as you see fit.

- Find visual symbols for the problem you're working on. Anything from the obvious (a photograph of the girlfriend who just left you, your work-clothes draped on a chair, your overloaded credit card propped in front of you) to the arcane (a photo of a certain kind of flower, which reminds you of your grandmother who is driving you crazy just now). Look at the symbol from time to time to see if it still triggers you.

- Do nothing: don't write it down. It'll still work. Reread the bit where I warn you that you'll forget the problem you started with, and that you'll decide that WHH doesn't work all that well after all. Say, "Ha, ha! You're wrong, I do remember!"

Step 2: Magnify the emotion if you can. Where does it sit in your body? Or: if you are starting from a body sensation, magnify that. What's the emotion inside it?

We're so used to avoiding pain: we skirt around it, we shove it aside, we look elsewhere. We cope.

To heal, however, we must do the opposite: face the discomfort, sink into it, embrace it. Feel the emotion fully, just as it is. As you sink into it, notice where it is in your body: all over? Enveloping you? In your throat, your chest, your back? In your hands, just above your head? Put as much as possible of your awareness in the area where the emotion is. Pay attention to the body sensations that go with this emotion. Is it tightness, burning, a sense of pressure? A sense of emptiness or blankness? Whatever it is, magnify that as well.[14]

"But I just feel blank"

Sink into the blank feeling just as if it was any other emotion. Where is the blank situated in your body? Just be in it: it will soon transform into another emotion.

"But I don't feel any emotions"

This is quite common. At each workshop I've attended, there was at least one person who didn't feel emotions right away when thinking about something that bothered him or her. Typically, this person has felt frustrated whenever he or she attended workshops about healing. If you're in this boat, take heart: it could be excellent news. It's possible that you're already in the Inner Peace state. This happens when your mind and

[14] This simple little technique of 'magnification' is adapted from Gay and Kathlyn Hendricks's excellent book on body-centred therapy, *At the Speed of Life.* You will see more ways to integrate elements from body-centred therapies with WHH in Chapter 6.

heart are functioning in harmony. People who are in Inner Peace don't have an emotional block. The past simply doesn't trigger them. When they focus on something that bothers them, however, they experience various types of body discomfort, an unease or a tightening or a vague ache.

If this is your case, start with the physical discomfort. Where is it in your body? Sink into it. If you feel tightness and can't relax it, make it tighter instead. Stay inside the discomfort until an emotion arises. Now you're ready for Step 3.

"But I really really don't feel any emotions"

Some people simply don't have much emotional range or intensity. Some kind of block usually causes this. I've experimented a bit with this problem. I'm finding out that one doesn't need very intense emotions at all to heal successfully. Consider this session transcript:

> Mark starts off by warning me that, except for some brief periods in his life, he's always been 'flat' emotionally. "The usual healing techniques take me nowhere," he says. "Nothing works." Like many unemotional types, Mark is married to a woman who is his opposite in that respect. The couple have a subconscious agreement that she will be the one to emote for both of them. One ancillary problem, then, is that Mark has misconceptions about emotions: he thinks emotions can only be the fiery, dramatic stuff that his wife does.
>
> I have him start from physical sensations. "When you think about your problem, what happens in your body?"
>
> "There's is a tightness in my chest. That's all there is."
>
> "Okay. Just move your awareness into the tightness... What is it like in there?"
>
> "I can't relax into it."
>
> "Fine. Just be inside the tightness exactly as it is. Make sure you're inside your body, not watching it from outside. If anything, try making it even a tiny bit tighter."
>
> "I somehow know I'm afraid. I can't *feel* it, you understand: I just seem to know that fear is what's in here."

That was enough. The session teetered precariously on the edge of unreality every step of the way, with very faint sensations and just shadows of emotions, mostly just *knowing about the emotion,* but that was enough! Mark and other clients completed healings successfully on these sketchy bits of information. Emotions are not necessarily earth shaking. For some people, they feel almost like thoughts.

If you've given all this a few tries and are getting no results at all, you might have a condition that really does block all emotions. A certified WHH therapist might be able to help you.

Step 3: Recall other times when you felt exactly this way. It won't necessarily be the same kind of incident: you're looking for the same type of emotion and body sensation. Choose the earliest incident you can recall, even if it doesn't seem to make sense.

Remember COEX systems? That's what this step is about. So we're looking for events that hold the same atmosphere: in Mark's session above, he looked for moments when he felt the same sort of tightness together with the same sort of fear. There might not be much of a logical thread between the problem that you started from and the earlier events. Rather, there is a certain emotional flavour that ties the events together. Trust your instinct on this one. Scanning those past events often feels more like free-association than regression.

In fact, regressing is easy: we do it all the time. Think of this situation: you're having to give a speech in front of a group of coworkers. Suddenly you go blank. Part of you sighs, "Oh no, not again!" The woman looking at you over her glasses in the first row looks *just* like your grade 3 teacher, the time you tried to fake a presentation on dinosaurs.

You've guessed it: you're in regression. You're not in front of a group of intelligent, compassionate adults. This is not a happy party speech you've agreed to make. You're being *judged*. And you're *failing*. Your very life is in the balance!

Now, if you decided to heal this particular event, you wouldn't have to go through the time last month when you rose to make a toast and forgot the host's name, and the time you faced the driving examiner, and the 23 other times you forgot or misplaced a concept or an instruction. By returning to the earliest event you can recall, and healing it completely, you can get rid of the emotional charge *for the whole stack*. More: as you get the regression ball rolling, if you sit without judgement or expectation, you will naturally regress further, to a place you won't recognize, but where the same shame, panic and tightness in the throat are present. Most likely it will be a pre-birth moment when your tiny self had an important biological task to accomplish and somehow lost track of a key element.

In their first sessions, most people don't allow themselves to perceive prenatal images. This doesn't mean that they didn't regress that far: if, using advanced techniques, I merge my consciousness with theirs, I often find prenatal sensations and images. I've had clients describing in living detail a sense of pressure on their heads, a sense of an endless tunnel and of leaving everything that they knew, and insisting that they were reliving a high school moment. I simply instruct them to consider the later images as metaphors and be open to the idea that they might actually be reliving a much, much earlier trauma. People still seem to get lasting changes from these sessions. With practice, they eventually sense more and more information from earlier events.

Some fortunate people actually perceive the trauma stack as an out-of-body image, and as an actual stack or string of shapes. Others will be in-body in a comparatively recent trauma, then spontaneously flip into an earlier event every few seconds or minutes... If you experience something like this, let yourself go to the earliest possible trauma. Keep flipping down the stack, into the past, until it seems like you can go no further.

"But I can't remember anything from long ago"

You can do this step even if you don't remember much of your past. Even an event from a few days ago will do fine. It'll get the regression ball rolling.

Not all COEXes lead before birth, either. A trauma stack could have originated last week - especially if there was a physical injury involved. Every session is different; there's no right or wrong way about this.

This step may indeed be the most misunderstood part of this technique. Students often witness their peers' sessions, then come out believing that, since they don't get those photographic prenatal images or don't have conscious recall before their birth, they will be unable to regress far enough to make the healing worthwhile. This is a regrettable belief. I suspect that all Step 3 really does is get your inner critic out of the way for the first few times you regress, giving it the impression that *it* guides you to the past, until you're familiar enough with the technique to trust that whenever you tune in to distressing feelings, you're *already* in the past. Step 3 also takes care of the events that *are* within your conscious recall or perception, if there are any, saving you the trouble of reliving each of them on your way.

In fact, after practising for a while, people often end up omitting this step altogether. They become used to the fact that whenever they feel triggered, they're already reliving a past trauma. After a while, you too will jump straight into the distant past simply by paying attention to the traumatic sensations. The second example at the end of this chapter shows a session where we omitted Step 3.

In short, then, Step 3 accomplishes several things: it allows you to bypass some of the events you *do* recall, leading you to the earliest in your memory; it allows your logical mind to get out of the way, and to believe it is controlling the movement into the past; it sets the intention to go right back to the origin of the trauma, and acts as a reminder to any part of you that can use it, consciously or subconsciously, of its navigating instructions - *down, wayyy back.*

Step 4: Place your hand on your chest to remind yourself to stay inside your body. If you see yourself 'out there', merge with the image of yourself until there's only one 'you'. This is the most important step.

This is one of the key differences between WHH and other regression therapies. If you are not *in your body in the past*, if you sense it from a dissociated state, you will still see or sense information from that moment. You will also feel emotions from that moment, or at least emotions *about* that moment. It will all seem utterly convincing. But the most you'll get is an intellectual understanding of what happened then. You'll come out with compassion for yourself, perhaps, and acceptance, and insights about your patterns, and all those good things. But the trauma pattern, frozen in the moment when you originally dissociated from your body, will still be intact. You'll understand why you act it out, but you'll still act it out.

The occasional amazing results from other therapies happen because some people instinctively do go back to their body in regression. Sometimes the regression is deliberate, as in the case of breathwork therapy; sometimes it's accidental or an unacknowledged side effect of the therapy: for example, a good bodywork session often throws us in regression. (There are ways to exploit this, which I'll discuss in Chapter 6.)

To merge correctly with the 'out-of-body' image, bring the image to yourself and put it on like a sweater. Sometimes there's much fear involved. If you run into difficulties, use the Loving-Yourself technique described in Chapter 2: love yourself exactly as you are, with no agenda to change. Once you feel the love, try merging again. Relaxing your diaphragm, throat and jaw also helps.

There are trickier ways to be out of our body: sometimes I sense something that seems to be other than me: a monster, a big monolith, anything. *These things, seen in regression, are also me.* I merge with them in the same way: become the monster or the monolith or what-have-you. Then I scan myself for new emotions and body sensations.

Another way we stay covertly out of the experience is to run to another area of our body. If, for example, the pain is in your heart and you consider it from the point of view of your mind, staying 'above' it, it is unlikely to release. Move as much of your awareness as possible *inside* the area of discomfort, and experience the frozen moment from within it.[15]

Step 5: **Love yourself in this moment in the past. Stay in the moment, focusing into any area that's injured, feeling the emotions and the body sensations, with no agenda to change anything. Love yourself exactly as you are. Relive this frozen moment from your past.**

This is the core of the healing. This is the healing itself: you need to relive now the moments that were unsafe to feel then.

No matter how bad it is, resist the urge to 'do something to fix it': yes, it's tempting to try throwing white light at it, to reach over to yourself, console yourself and try to make it all better... people usually end up outside their body's past image when they do this, and the healing stalls. Doing "magic" on it—trying to wash away the trauma with light and such things—seems to bring temporary relief, but the trauma usually rebuilds later, because the core emotion remains unhealed.

Some things do help to speed the healing:

- As soon as you have an emotion and a body sensation together, use the Loving-Yourself technique.

---

[15] An alternate way to accomplish the same thing is to spread the discomfort to your whole body, bit by bit. Example: you have pain in your solar plexus. Let it spread and fill your chest and over to your back. It continues to spread down your torso to you navel, then lower belly, neck, arm, down your legs and up to your head, until finally your whole body feels it uniformly.

- It may help to pull in the sense of a greater presence, or of white or golden light, not to push away or cleanse away the trauma, but to be with it: to witness it, to be part of the background.
- If this is prenatal, it may also help to remember that your mother is around you, and, around her, the Earth itself. (Of course, if you're the sperm, pre-conception, it's your father who is there.) Keep your attention on the injury and on your own emotions but, if you can, widen your awareness slightly to encompass what's around you. Most of the instances of stalled healings are because we're missing a component of the situation.

Step 6: Stay in this moment until something changes: often a few words will pop out, having to do with the beliefs that you anchored in yourself in that trauma moment. The picture changes: another emotion arises, or an earlier situation arises. Repeat steps 4, 5 and 6 for the new emotion/body sensation. It doesn't matter if you don't know the story, if you don't know where you are: feel the emotion, feel where it is in your body, love yourself. Keep going further and further back in time in this way.

Traumas often contain a short phrase—a belief, true or false, that comes out at the moment when the trauma releases. When this happens, if you have enough privacy, say the words aloud. Whispering them is just as effective as screaming them—more, actually, because screaming takes you out of the tension and attempts to throw it outwards. Having the emotion, body sensation and phrase come together seems to bring a more complete release of the trauma. Keep whispering the words until they hold no charge. Remember to stay in your body.

At this point in the healing, trying to make sense of 'the story' is more likely to hamper the process than to help it. Leave aside your desire to understand, for now. After you complete the session, while you write your notes, the story often comes together. That is the proper time to analyse what happened and speculate on meanings.

Even after thousands of hours of practice, in an average session I often have no clue where I've regressed to until quite late into the process. When it comes, the knowledge isn't necessarily in the form of visual images; sometimes it's a tactile sensation ("I feel all wiggly and there's a sense of a big sphere I'm attracted to nearby") or just a vague knowing. Often I recognise a moment only because I've been there so many times ("It feels birth-ish.")

Yes, you will certainly hear of people who get precise visuals in regression, but, paradoxically, to get more details about where you are, your best bet isn't to strain your eyes but to pay detailed attention to your tactile sensations. Is there a weight, a pull, a sense of compression, of stretching? What is the texture, the temperature? Just accept things as they are. This is the quickest way to release traumas.

I'd say that in about a third of my sessions, I never do find out where I was. I don't worry about it anymore, because the process still works—I finish the session feeling better about the issue I started with.

Sometimes I've found out where I was, long afterwards. For example, in a series of sessions in 2002, I found myself feeling like the mythic primal mud, hit by lightning. Had I regressed all the way to the beginning of life? I just wrote my notes, keeping the actual experience separate from my speculations. A year later, I heard that another Institute member had had the same experience. Another six months later someone with unusual abilities mapped some very early developmental moments that were earlier than we had thought it possible to remember. They included… a moment when we feel like the primal mud hit by lightning. (The theory of lightning on mud as the first source of life has fallen out of favour lately. One can understand, however, how the image would capture our imagination if we've each lived such a moment as germ cells before we were conceived.)

Step 7: When nothing remains except calm, peace and a weightless feeling, you are done. If the moment you healed is before birth, you should also feel large and bright. Stay in the moment for a few minutes, to make sure no further trauma arises. If one does, go back to Step 4.

The expansion of full healing can be quite startling the first time you get there! It's normal; it's the desirable result. Enjoy it for a while. You'll regain a more normal size as you come out of the regression. Some people retain a sense of expansion and lightness for a while. This means you've healed an important event in your early development. See also the section on transpersonal experiences and peak states in the next chapter.

Step 8: Check your work. There should be no out-of-body image when you look back at the traumatic moment. Look at the description

you wrote at the start of the process. It should no longer trigger you. If any emotions besides calm, peace and lightness are present, return to Step 4, or plan to return at a later session.

To be really thorough, you should also check the trauma moments you perceived on your way. There should be no out-of-body image of any of them. If there is, there might have been a physical injury that needs individual healing, so return to step 4 with it.

Some people have a tightly-packed, interwoven trauma load, and rarely feel large and bright. (I'm one of them; I feel it 2 or 3 times a year; it lasts about ten seconds, then the next issue comes up...) This doesn't mean their issue isn't healed, however. Check if you're calm, specifically, about the issue you started with—the issue you wrote down. Give yourself credit for work well done. Return for the rest another time.

Here are some transcripts of actual sessions, showing how those theoretical steps fit together in practice. It all looks so ideal in those step-by-step methods. Reality is much messier. (And transcripts give no clues about the time elapsed, the many quiet intervals spent on the actual hard work, the reliving of the traumas.) As you work through your first sessions, don't get overly hung up on each step. Rather, *focus on the general principles: feel the emotions and body sensations, stay in your body in the past, love yourself, and continue long enough.*

The first session, although the client's problems seemed very complex, was in fact straightforward and had a very satisfying ending. Note the variation on the Loving Yourself technique that we used when Julie's feelings were so overwhelming that she couldn't love herself. Also note that "it feels red," while unconventional, is a perfectly valid emotion.

> Julie had a severe childhood accident that left her with a brain injury. Her ability to read is compromised; remembering is difficult, fine motor skills are affected. She has chronic neck pain.
>
> During this session, she wanted to work on her marital difficulties. "It's like I'm addicted to needing my husband. Also I'm angry because he doesn't take proper care of my belongings. He borrows things and breaks them. I keep feeling I should leave him."
>
> I did the writing for her. I read the above sentences back. "What's the dominant emotion now?"
>
> "It's sadness."
>
> "And where is that sadness?"

"In my heart."

"Okay. Recall any other event in the past when you felt the same sort of sadness in your heart."

..."It reminds me of when my mother died."

"Okay. Just go to that moment of sadness around your mother's death."

"How do I do that?"

"Just remember being there. And when you have it, please describe the scene for me."

"It's all happening too fast, just like my marriage did. People are taking her out of the room, there's no time to take decisions, everything's rushed." [Her marriage happened a few years after her mother's death, so we stay with the earlier event. But her reference to it shows that both events are part of the same COEX system.]

"And where are you? Do you see that scene from inside your body?"

"No, I'm over there." [Points.]

"Okay. Just merge with yourself in the past. Look at that scene from the point of view of your twenty-year-old self."

"Okay. I'm there."

"What's the feeling now?"

"Still sadness. Lots of it."

"Is it still in your chest?"

"Yes. In my heart."

"Now just stay in the sadness in your heart. There's no need to change it, just love and accept yourself as you are in this moment."

"The sadness is stronger."

"Stay inside it, love yourself..."

[Growing panic] "I can't; it feels like my heart is shutting down."

"Try just lighting a tiny candle of love, right in the middle of your heart that is shutting down."

[Big release of ragged breaths.] ..."I see my mother's death again, but now it's peaceful..."

"Okay. Scan your body for any remaining sensations and emotions."

"The pain in my neck is acting up. It's the same pain I've had ever since the accident."

"Okay. Just put your awareness in that pain in your neck."

"I'm afraid to go there."

"And where is that fear?"

"Still in my heart."

"Love yourself exactly as you are, with this fear in your heart."

..."It's gone. Should I try to go in my neck again?"

"Yes please."

"It hurts and it feels... red. I don't know how to explain it."

"Fine. Just stay in that red feeling in your neck. No need to make sense of it, no need to change it. Just love and accept yourself exactly as you are."

..." Hey! It's just turned green!"
"How's your neck pain?"
[Excited] "It's almost gone; that's the least pain I've had for a long, long time."
"Great. Now think about your husband, about your feeling of addiction to needing him, and your anger."
"I just feel neutral about this now. It feels like my stuff is just stuff, it's not that important if it gets broken or not, you know? They're just things."
We decided to end the session there. Her goal had been to address her marital difficulties, and she was calm, peaceful and light about that. She noticed how vividly green my garden seemed to her. The next week I saw her in a public place, alone, looking relaxed and happy. Before this, I'd only seen her go out closely accompanied by her husband or a family member.

This second session illustrates the trouble-shooting for three problems: the inability to use the Loving Yourself technique, a temporarily stuck healing due to a 'copy' and, later, the appearance of something that seems external to the student's body. More about 'copies' in the next chapter, but again, when the healing became stuck, the simple act of encompassing the mother into the scene immediately clarified the situation and that particular trauma released within seconds.

This student, although he was new to WHH, was familiar with other regression therapies, so we skipped Step 3 in this session.

It was Ovid's first session. I started by teaching him the Loving Yourself technique. We were just at the first part: imagine something that's very easy to love. Ovid chose something suitably unthreatening: a rose.
Paula: Now just love this rose until that love feels nice and strong.
Ovid: My first reaction is, 'This is painful.'

We decided to make this the topic of this first session. Where loving oneself was required, I simply substituted something less threatening: the concept of accepting and honouring oneself and the situation.
Paula: Where is that sense that 'love is painful'?
Ovid: In my belly. It's fear.
P: Magnify that fear a little... Now just accept and honour yourself, exactly as you are, with that fear. There's no agenda to change anything.
O: [After a while, heaves sigh.] It's shifted. There's still pain, along my sternum.
P: Just let yourself sink into that pain... What's the emotion inside it?
O: It's betrayal.
...
O: [Distressed.] I was told to grow strong, and now it's a bad thing!

...

O: I was a big baby, more than ten pounds. Feels like I was told to grow and be strong and it was a good thing... until birth! My mom had a hell of a time.

P: How is it now?

O: There's a whole mix of feelings, it's complicated.

P: Still in your chest?

O: Yes. Maybe elsewhere as well, I can't tell just now.

P: Honour and accept yourself with this whole mix of feelings. No need to select one; just be with them all.

[Healing going nowhere for a few minutes. I check for the most likely reason, a 'copy', by giving the following cue.]

P: Your mother is around you, possibly giving birth to you. Are any of these her feelings?

O: ...It's complicated. Certainly the fear is hers... It's my pain and my belligerence.

O: [sudden onrush of emotions] I did it wrong!

P: That's the belief anchored in this injury. Repeat it to yourself until it doesn't hold any charge anymore.

O: ... The pain is easing up. Feels brighter in here.

P: Try loving that rose again. [I'm refocusing the session back to the problem we started with to check for progress, and to re-trigger him if it's needed.]

O: The emotions that were in the foreground are now in the background.

P: And what's in the foreground?

O: Chatter. All around my torso, inside and out. Like a whole lot of people nattering.

P: Pay attention to the chatter. What's the content?

O: The theme is don't lose yourself, it isn't safe.

P: Become the one who says this. Widen your awareness, just a bit, just enough to take in the part of the chatter that's outside your torso. Become the whole area who says this.

[When an emotion seems just outside or partly outside ourselves, it often belongs to our placenta, which is part of us, of course. As soon as he's widened his sense of self to encompass it, Ovid 's sensations changed drastically.]

O: I feel big, defensive and angry.

P: Okay. Just honour and accept yourself as big, defensive and angry. Just be this defensive and angry self.

O: The core message is that love is a distraction from survival. "If you love completely you will die."

P: How's the emotional punch of that phrase now?

O: It's gone. The whole scene has changed! I feel brighter. Calmer. I'm this big placenta surrounding and embracing like a big comfort blanket.

P: Try loving that rose again.

O: ...It's just a rose...

[Ovid completes the Loving Yourself exercise with ease.]

O: I was getting a taste of what really is a whole ocean out there... a whole ocean of love perhaps.

Good News for Those of Us who Live in Small Apartments: Feeling Emotions vs. Expressing Emotions

A friend of mine, who's built like a chest freezer and had a childhood's worth of multiple accidents and illnesses and a truckload of other early traumas, tells the story of helping his father tear down a condemned building. There was nothing of value in the rambling two-story house, so my friend's father handed him a long wrecker's bar and told him that this would be a good place to work out some of his anger. My friend attacked the job, using rage as fuel, until, after two hours of mayhem, he had cut the building neatly in half. Had he exhausted his anger? Not one bit. The physical activity allowed the release of endorphins, so he felt better for a while, but the relief was short lived. My friend is justifiably worried when he goes to see a shrink who suggests that he pound on some pillows to 'get it out of his system'. He knows what he's capable of.

There's a difference between feeling emotions and expressing them. I've relived plenty of traumas where the crowbar approach seemed like just the thing. I would have made short work of my nice new house. Instead, I did the more difficult thing: I stayed on the couch, knowing my anger, feeling it head on. If I grab a wrecker's bar, I don't *feel* the anger: I transmute it into kinetic energy. If I sit quietly and stay with it... there follow a few very nasty moments. Then something changes. Anger, as many therapists know, often acts as a secondary emotion. This means that the trauma, perceived from a dissociated standpoint, feels like anger, but the emotion *inside* the trauma is not necessarily the same. If one simply sits in one's body and feels it long enough, anger soon gives way to other emotions: fear, shame, loneliness... One can rip through a few houses before going there. Or else one can sit quietly with it, *inside it*, for about one minute.

The same goes for other emotions. I can't stop my tears from falling when I feel sadness, but I do have the choice on whether to actually unleash the screams or to open my throat wide and make no actual sound. When I started using this technique, I had some safe space and I really went for it. But something weird started happening: at each session, I got worked up into huge rushes of adrenaline. Sometimes the session itself would make me pop out of my body: the session itself was traumatic, and then I had to go back to heal *that*. In a few weeks I became an adrenaline freak. My mentor thought it was all a bit much. I put it down to cultural differences: what would a man of Scots descent know about emotions anyway?

Finally, I understood what he meant: I was letting the traumas take me over. I was letting the emotions become bigger than me. The problem wasn't so much about noise or intensity of feeling; it was about deciding who's in charge. I was losing control of the sessions and this was unnecessary and even dangerous. Once I acknowledged this, I learned to identify a part of myself — for lack of a better term I call it my Higher Self — who could stay in the driver's seat. *The Basic Whole-Hearted Healing Manual* says, "Imagine a bright light in your chest. This light is you, and it is whole." I'll add this: this light is your Higher Self. The one who remains in charge. This part of you is bigger than the traumas. On very rare occasions, it might feel overwhelmed, and this is the sure marker of a generational trauma. (More about this in the next chapter.)

In general, apart from copious nose blowing, and a few moans when the going gets really rough, my sessions are now on the quiet side. And just in time, too: a few weeks after I finally understood how to feel deeply without letting my emotions run away on me, I moved to a neighbourhood where the houses are much closer together. No one has called the police yet.

Chapter 4

Special Situations in Healing

This chapter revisits the second part of the 'WHH memory aids' and discusses each occurrence in more detail, with some examples and the odd exercise thrown in. Almost every session involves one or two of these special occurrences, and the general principles apply: stay in your body in the past, keep track of both the physical and emotional components of the injury, and love yourself exactly as you are, with no agenda to change anything.

We saw earlier that whenever a healing stalls, it means we're missing some component of the trauma. The purpose of this chapter is to help you identify some of the missing pieces. It's not necessary to keep them all in mind as you embark on a regression. Rather, stick to the basic principles, look up whatever strange thing appeared, and learn gradually, letting the lessons of each session coach you for the next.

To heal a trauma with a regression therapy, you have to be inside your body, inside the trauma, in the past. And really, all these 'special situations' are about spotting and remedying the tricky ways we have of not being in-body, of avoiding the core of the trauma: we hide it in a hole, shroud it in numbness, project it onto some scary being out there, mask it with someone else's emotions, fail to see it as extending up our genetic line... So this is still basic WHH, and it's still about being inside the trauma in the past, and about welcoming home these lost bits of ourselves.

Working with Prenatal Memories

The first time I regressed to a prenatal memory, I had no idea where I was. For years before learning to use WHH, I had heard that our problems were all about our childhoods, so while trying to cope with abuse issues I did my best to recall early childhood events. And almost every time I tried to do this, I would end up in a light-grey, warm place, where there were no emotions except a vague sadness. It felt relatively safe, and I was wearing some sort of hooded cloak, which I came to call my cloak of sadness. I had no idea what this meant, and nobody I asked knew, either.

Imagine my puzzlement when, at my third self-taught WHH session, I found myself again in this same place! There being no emotions to speak of, I couldn't do anything with it and stalled there.

Next session, same thing. And the next. That's when I gave Grant McFetridge a call. He offered to guide me through a session.

I promptly returned to my grey cloak of sadness. Still no feeling besides this vague, vague sadness. This is when Grant told me I was in my mom's uterus.

It turns out that fetal consciousness is very different from our everyday perceptions. And that prenatal traumas always have some physical injury as a component. For example, as Grant explains in *the Basic WHH Manual* (p. 32), rejection by one's mother is not by itself a cause of womb trauma. The fetus may not like it, but at least the rejection won't 'stick' and wreck his life. However, if the feelings of rejection happen during an event that also physically injures the fetus, the rejection becomes part of the trauma. The principal causes of injury include toxic foods ingested by the mother, smoking, alcohol, medications that cross the placental barrier, electric shock, painful noise, and direct injury from falls or rough sexual contact. By far the most common cause of physical injury is lack of oxygen to the fetus. Stress and smoking, notably, restrict the flow of oxygen through the placenta.

During the few years I had spent in survival mode, I had taught myself to disregard physical pain. Not that I didn't feel it, but it simply was something I didn't have the luxury to attend to. So it took a bit of coaching for me to focus on the physical pain. After I had located it, I learned to sink into it instead of avoiding it or skirting it, and behold, the emotional component of the trauma came out of hiding. This is why, in my teaching, I focus on the need to attend to the physical component of traumas right from the start.

Surprise, surprise: a tiny fetus doesn't *feel* tiny. It just feels like *me*. An egg doesn't feel like just one cell: it feels like me, feeling like a planet. A sperm doesn't feel microscopic: it feels like me with my legs fused into a tail and a wiggly way of being. In fact, when a prebirth memory is completely healed, one feels *very* large, and bright, in addition to the usual calm, peaceful and lightweight feelings.

There was another surprise in store during that session. I was lying on some cushions with my eyes closed, and suddenly I felt a very threatening, very physical presence, inches behind me. Great, I thought, here's this man I trust for a session and now he's attacking me? What came out of my mouth was just an imperious "What are you doing??" - but Grant's voice replied peacefully from the other side of the room, "I'm just sitting right here."

"Then what's this behind my back? Feels like someone there."

"Oh, that's your placenta. It's part of you, you know."

"No way! Placenta is part of the mother!"

"No it's not. Just merge with it and learn how it feels."

I had to heal some fear and resistance before I could do this. But Grant was right: my placenta is part of me. That cloak of sadness was my placenta all along. The amniotic sac is also a part of the placental awareness, and so is the umbilical cord. Whenever there's a prenatal trauma, there's likely to be a placental component to it.

To feel your placenta, once you have regressed to a time before birth, do one of the following: envision the cord exiting your navel and slowly move your awareness along that until you feel the whole envelope of the placenta and amniotic sac around you; or else widen your awareness to encompass the first few inches around your body. Yes, it's perfectly all right to fake it at first.

I often have a sort of knowing about which side of my body my placenta sits on. Once I have that, if I have difficulty merging into my placenta, I pretend to 'trade places' with it: either move back an inch or two in the couch, like backing into it, if it is behind me, or else I turn around to face myself, as it were, if it feels as if it's in front of me. [16]

---

[16] In the time zone around the moment of birth, the placenta feels as if it has to die (in fact, it doesn't really die; its essence joins that of the new baby). For some people, this may evoke surprisingly strong suicidal feelings. DO NOT explore this time zone without competent supervision. See also the footnote on page 126 in Chapter 5.

Working with Egg and Sperm Memories

One of the more controversial aspects of our work is the concept that consciousness predates the moment of conception. A few people access egg and sperm memories right in their first session. Seen from a dissociated state, the egg looks like a planet or the moon or a ball of light. If you merge with it, it feels like you, and somehow all your body parts fit into this ball. It also sometimes feels like a young version of your mother. The sperm often shows up as fish-like or tadpole-like, or, in some traumatic instances, snake-like. If you merge with it, again your body's geography somehow fits into it. Your legs might feel fused, or else the tail might feel like it's in your mid-back. You might also feel like a young version of your father.

You should suspect egg or sperm trauma any time the physical injury seems to be on just one side of your body, stopping at the midline. Usually the egg is represented on the left side and the sperm on the right, though sometimes this is reversed.

The egg and sperm often sustain injuries on their way to conception. And conception itself is a traumatic event for nearly everyone. A lot of couples' issues are attempts to replay and resolve conception traumas.

Heal egg and sperm memories just as you would heal womb traumas. Make sure to include the body sensations in your healing: there is always a physical component to the injury.

Working with Precellular Memories

Yes, our consciousness starts very early indeed... Occasionally, as you follow a trauma stack to its origin, the images stop looking like anything biological. You might see a wide horizon line with a stripy sky, some quivering blobs or cubes of jelly, a sort of fountain... These are metaphors we make up, trying to translate into coherent images what we call the precellular environment: our world before the egg and sperm are constructed. In this world, each of the brains already has an analogue: an organelle that will assume that particular brain's function in the single cell of the egg or sperm, and that will eventually develop into that brain.

These situations are healed just the same way as all the others: go into the "body" of whatever you were at that time, and experience fully what happened until you feel large and bright.

Emptiness or Blank Feeling

There is a big difference between feeling peaceful and feeling blank. Sensations of calm, peace and lightness are the goal of all our healing sessions. Blankness, in contrast, is an absence of feelings, or rather a way we use to block emotions and sensations that are too threatening.

Our approach is to treat blankness itself as an emotion or body sensation.

Where in your body is the emptiness or blankness located? Move your attention into it. Love yourself for being empty or blank. Be the blank. The hidden emotion will soon arise. Heal it the usual way.

Sometimes it takes a few minutes for the blankness to reveal the other sensations hidden inside it. To speed the process, try pressing your hand briefly and gently into the blank area. Some people get a flash-like image of the traumatic moment when they do this. It can be a visual image, a tactile impression or any kind of 'knowing' about where you were and what was happening at the moment of injury. You don't need a technicolor view of the scene in order to heal. For example, a student who is affected by cataracts wanted to heal his petrifying fear about getting treatment. Whenever he tried to evoke the fear with the intention of healing it, he would suddenly go blank and feel nothing. So he tried this technique, closing his eyes and pressing his fingers briefly and *very* gently into the one that was the most affected. What he got was just a split-second impression of a woman's face. We did a bit of digging about the image. Was it anyone he recognized? A lover, his mother? No. Did it feel like a feminine version of him? Not particularly.

As it turned out, he was indeed seeing an aspect of himself.

I had him visualise whatever he could remember about the woman's face, then identify any feelings or sensations that surfaced. He suddenly felt fear in his face. Before long he identified the event: he was the sperm, heading for a face-first collision with the egg's surface. The blankness at the thought of having anyone touch his eyes was a re-enactment of the fear of that conception moment, and the woman's face was a metaphorical image of him as an egg. The image had seemed impossibly vague, but it still triggered the relevant feelings.

Holes

Experientially, this is a more dramatic version of the 'emptiness' described above. Holes feel like a distinct lack, deficiency or emptiness. Some people see them as a black, seemingly bottomless cavity with its opening flush with their skin. There may be a rim around it. Once I saw one that looked like a manhole, complete with a ladder! We often make up metaphors this way, converting unknown sights into something familiar.

Holes seem to be caused by particularly severe prenatal injuries. Recent experimentation leads us to speculate that holes might even be associated with genetic damage.

We put a lot of effort into concealing these injuries from our conscious awareness. We try to cover them and fill them in all sorts of bizarre ways. For that reason, holes often appear when a healing session is well under way. Often my first clue of a hole's existence is a sort of shivery tightness over a large area of my skin. If the hole is less defended, I feel that dreadful emptiness.

Some people feel like the emptiness comes from everywhere at once. If that happens to you, run your hands lightly all over your skin. The location of the hole should become more precise.

When you sense that kind of emptiness, the last thing you want to do is to go anywhere near it, but this is what you must do, and immediately. Focus yourself into the lack as completely as possible. Put as much of 'yourself' as possible into that hole. Stay *in your body, in the hole.* Feel that awful emptiness and that awful darkness, love yourself exactly as you are, and wait it out. Resist any impulse to 'do' anything to it, like flood it with white light and so on. Make sure you explore the whole extent of it, slowly and gently 'feeling' around for its boundaries — some holes have two or more branches. Pay special attention to physical sensations.

As you move around the hole, once you get past the empty feeling, various strong emotions will surface. There are typically several traumas or aspects of traumas in each hole. Whenever this happens, do a freeze-frame at that location and moment and heal the emotion and body sensation. Keep healing everything you feel, no matter how impossible this seems. Holes often contain secondary emotions, such as anger, shame and the feeling of evil. Love and accept yourself for whatever comes up. There are often other emotions like fear and loneliness hidden in those. The feeling of evil is just an emotion, like any other emotion.

There is no reason to run away from it, and every reason to stay with it, relive it, and heal it.

Every time I heal a hole, there comes a moment when I think, 'this will never go away, it'll never heal, it'll never be over.' It comes like clockwork and now I recognize it as an indication that I'm about two thirds of the way through.

If the trauma doesn't release, try the technique described in the last section: press your hand gently into the area of the hole. A very brief image or sensation will appear, perhaps guiding you to an overlooked aspect of the problem. Some people find that using direct pressure on the area allows the healing to happen when nothing else does. Experiment with various kinds of gentle touch.

As the trauma releases, the hole becomes lighter and seems to fill in. Some people sense an intense feeling of sacredness in the area. Continue healing until all is calm, peaceful and light.

Here is a note from Tal, explaining how people with good 'visual' perceptions can heal holes. This does not correspond to anything within my experience, but some of you will certainly encounter this type of perception. She writes:

> "Two ways I know of healing holes:
>
> "1. Let yourself drop down the hole. When you stop dropping you will be around half way down and you will see an image of the trauma. Enter it and heal it like any other trauma. There may be further regression, though very often this is the earliest trauma on the COEX string.
>
> "2. Some people do not get an image at the mid-point. For those, it is recommended to continue downward. This is a struggle, because there is a force pushing upwards. When you reach the bottom it will look like a sandy floor. Sit there and accept and heal all physical and emotional sensations coming up until you are calm, peaceful and lightweight. At the endpoint the hole will flood with light from below, though sometimes it comes from the sides, and you will rise and find yourself on the outside of your body. It is important to stay on the floor and focus on healing sensations and emotions. The light will come on its own. "

Next is an example from my notebooks. My first hole was by far the worst one I ever healed. Most of them are not nearly this bad, but the example illustrates the need for acceptance no matter what you experience.

This was part of a whole sequence on my own birth. The traumas had been very severe throughout the sequence. I would start every day from present-time triggers and end up revisiting the next instalment of the past.

> Trigger: I'm annoyed at myself for trying to ingratiate myself to someone I'm attracted to. First waypoint: similar situation a year ago. Second waypoint: almost the same scenario, maybe 10 years ago. End point: I don't know where, maybe I'm already born, the pain is in my back, not placental, and I've felt this sort of pain before. Defence: loud music playing in my head.
>
> A *big black hole*. I go in and it's gigantic, it sinks from my shoulder blade all the way to my rectum, then down my right thigh. It's *scary*. I go in as well as I can, not sure if I should feel it as a cavity inside my body or step into it, so I do a bit of each. As I chart its depths, its boundaries start to tingle.
>
> What I find after a fearful while: this is the place that twists all my good intentions and makes them awful, ingratiating, manipulative, sideways-lying, white lies, half-truths. I try to be straight and good, and through here everything comes out crooked and I know it, and moreover crooked to my advantage and I know it. It's twisted and putrescent in here and it's just awful.
>
> White light comes into my third eye: a stream. I push it back forcefully, afraid that this terrible hole will twist and taint that, too.
>
> "I'm not a temple, never will be; light, you must stay away!"
>
> I work on my own, cleaning and closing the hole with my will. Then to my horror I realize that the lowest branch of it is getting sealed in, the foulness trapped while the hole closes itself like a living cave in a very bad movie. I get panicked thoughts about having to dig this foulness out of me with a knife. Now I understand about this man of my acquaintance who committed suicide because his body felt evil. If this felt trapped in you for good, you'd think you had no choice but to jump off a bridge.
>
> At last I remember: I can't *fix* this, I can just love myself as I am, love myself for being this way and for feeling this way... Relief!! The hole slowly opens up again; the trapped part becomes accessible. After a long while, some light comes in on its own, comfortable, making me laugh. I keep working at trying to love the unlovable.
>
> Suddenly, with no transition, I'm beached on my back on Mount Ararat: becalmed. I am here, I am born: I am human. The hole is completely gone.

There was a bit more to this session. I'll share the rest of those notes in the section on 'copies.'

'New' Physical Pain

Physical pain sometimes arises seemingly from nowhere during healing. Or chronic pain starts acting up unexpectedly. 'New' pain in this context means 'new in this session'; you may have felt it before. This pain may be from an earlier event that has not appeared in the picture yet, and has surfaced only enough for the physical component to be felt. Or is it a distraction?... Magnify the pain, and relax into it rather than trying to avoid it. Do this until you feel the emotion inside the pain. Figure out if it belongs with the problem by thinking back to the trigger you started from. What is happening to the injury you were working on until then? Is it gone? Which injury seems most relevant? Which injury seems earliest? Go with the earliest, the most relevant to the trigger, the most intense.

We tend to run away from physical pain, to work around it, to medicate it, to cope with it. But to access the trauma that causes the pain, we must do the opposite: we must go sit right in the middle of that pain. This is the only way to access the emotional component of the physical discomfort; and bringing together the emotion and physical sensation are the keys to healing. In most cases, sitting right in the middle of the pain and feeling its emotional content will actually greatly lessen the physical discomfort, after some initial nasty moments.

Fatigue falls under this heading too. Some fatigue is normal if you've been working on yourself for two hours, but a heavy, gluey tiredness fifteen minutes into the session is definitely a sign that some new trauma is arising.

Magnify the pain or discomfort, if you can stand that. Relax into it rather than trying to avoid it. Can't relax? Too tight? Then sit in the tightness... and if anything, make it just a little bit tighter. Do this until you feel the emotion inside the pain. Heal the emotion and physical sensation in the usual way.

In the example of Julie's session, at the end of last chapter, we see an example of chronic pain (from a car accident) starting to act up in the middle of a healing.

Copies

The greatest source of emotional distress for a baby during gestation may well be that he cannot tell his own feelings apart from his mother's. In the womb, our consciousness is vastly different from the everyday perceptions we are used to as grownups. We feel boundary-less, and it's sometimes impossible to sort out which sensations are whose. This is true for physical sensations but even more for emotions. The problem gets compounded when we suffer severe injuries: as we dissociate from the pain or 'pop out of our body', we may end up separated from ourselves but unknowingly merged with our mother (or our father, if this is a sperm memory), or anyone who's nearby. We have no way to tell the difference. So in this moment we end up feeling the parent's emotions *instead* of our own!

This may also happen after birth: out of a desire for closeness or protection, we adopt the emotions of people we feel close to: family, friends, anyone around us. [17]

To heal traumas completely, we must feel *our own* emotions and physical sensations. And by far the most common cause of a stuck healing is this phenomenon of 'copying.' We copy when we take someone else's sensations for our own. We can stay with these sensations until the cows come home and nothing changes, because we haven't yet accessed what *we* actually felt in that moment.

Some people can tell they're dealing with a copy because the emotions have someone else's tone in it. Grant writes:

> In my case, I could tell when I copied stuff from my dad, because the feeling had a sort of a Dad tone to it. It was much harder to tell in the case of my mother, because at birth I identified my emotional self with Mom, and this was reinforced growing up because she was my 'safe' parent. It's taken me a long time to get better at spotting 'mom' copies.[18]

I always suspect a copy whenever a trauma doesn't move within a few minutes. It's easy to check for one without disrupting the healing, so I try it as soon as I can remember (which is usually after 10 or more minutes of spinning my wheels and going nowhere. I'm better at spotting the situation in clients.)[19]

---

[17] There is, in fact, disagreement within the Institute about whether copies happen before or after birth or both. I've only seen them before birth, in myself and in several students and clients; on the other hand, Grant wrote as a note to this section, "Copies can happen, and usually do, after birth. Actually, I don't think they ever happen before birth." Which just goes to show you how fluid the details of this model still are. Be aware of the possibilities, and trust your own perceptions.

[18] *The Basic Whole-Hearted Healing Manual,* p. 26.

[19] From Grant: "In my experience, the most common cause for meridian tapping having no effect is because the feeling is a copy."

To check for a copy, do the following:

- Expand your awareness outwards a bit. If this seems impossible, simply ask yourself who is around you in the past moment you're healing. Does it feel like your Mom or your Dad? Just follow your gut feeling on that one. During very early events, before conception, we sometimes also feel one of our grandmothers (paternal or maternal); at other times, we are fully able to perceive the emotions of other people nearby. In the vast majority of cases, if the problem is before birth, our mother is the one we copy from.

- If you're dealing with a moment after your birth, ask yourself, who does this situation remind me of? Who was I with when I first felt this?

- Some people get full-blown images of their surroundings at this time. The rest of us can release copies just as easily, however: ask yourself, Is this feeling in my body really mine, or does it belong to this other person?

- Ovid's example at the end of last chapter shows a situation where the emotion was only partly copied. Sorting out which emotion belonged to whom sparked an instantaneous, drastic change. But in most cases we must ask, "If this emotion I'm stuck with right now belongs to this outside person, then what am *I* feeling?"

This may seem iffy on paper, but it's actually very easy when you're in the situation. I've never seen a student or client have any trouble recognizing his or her own emotions once it was pointed out that a person nearby may have been the source of the 'stuck' emotion.

Here is the rest of my notes from the session during which I found the big hole. It's one of the few instances where I copied physical sensations as well as emotions. But here, the simple intention to complete the picture was enough to release the copy. And the results were well worth the work.

> I'm beached on Mount Ararat, then. I say, This is who I am... I'm born now... This is who I am, an imperfect human. I'll have to just live, with my limitations...
>
> Boy, is this ever dreary. Is this ever bleak. Can this be all there is to a fully healed birth? I must be missing something...
>
> Twinge to my left shoulder. An injury I felt earlier in this birth sequence, remembered now. Arm heavy like a stone.
>
> "Wait a minute! *There* you are!" I say to the pain and the flat ordinary despair.
>
> My father's face floats into view. *It's his arm.* I've been feeling his arm! I don't need to ask what my *own* emotions are: I'm mad as hell, a joyous anger after all that grey.
>
> "Vale-of-tears, eh? That's *you*, the old-time religion! Père, take your luggage, and your devil too! And that's *my* arm, not yours!"
>
> I notice it's the left arm: his evil left arm, poor dear one, the one that got tied behind his back or hit with a ruler at school so he wouldn't write with it. The arm filled with their old-time religious guilt.
>
> The rest was more like house-cleaning, and thanking all the guest performers and helpers: Père, Mère, my own granddaughter, my paternal grandmother, the people in the present I had projected my problem on, and especially the Light, whatever it may be.
>
> Don't ask me about Light: I do not know what I am. I'm in this blessed state of having absolutely no way to judge myself. I am neither this nor that: just all the boundless possibility of a person. Everything seems easy.

Soul Stealing

Experientially, soul stealing feels like a more comprehensive version of copying, although it's done through a different brain (the heart makes copies, the body brain does soul stealing). As in copying, we take on someone else's emotions or body sensations, but in soul stealing the sensations are much more persistent and can intrude in our daily lives, sometimes causing severe disruption. A copy feels like a stuck emotion or sensation, but a soul piece is a trauma "dialoguing with you", to use Tal's description.

Here's Grant, writing in *The Basic Whole-Hearted Healing Manual*, page 57:

"...To understand [soul stealing] and what to do about it, you need to have some shamanic background along with more conventional experience.

"As a hypothesis, assume that your sense of 'I', of consciousness, is composed of a non-physical 'material' that is a small portion of the Creator itself. Shamans call this stuff 'soul'. During certain traumas, the pain is so bad that you actually eject a piece of yourself, along with the emotional memory of what happened, out of your body area, and it wanders around loose. In the shamanic tradition, this is called soul loss [see next section]. If a shaman brings yours back to you, they call it soul retrieval. If you've got somebody else's, this is called soul stealing [although you're certainly not aware of having 'stolen' anything!] In Christian terms, these soul pieces would probably be called entities or angels, depending on the emotional tone of the trauma that formed the piece. "

The most common manifestation of soul pieces is the voices or 'tapes' that many people keep hearing in their heads. Some people actually know whose voice it is, for example your mother's voice repeating over and over that you're no good and will never succeed. This is different from sub-vocalization or 'self-talk'. The voices are someone else's, and usually they are difficult to control. More severe forms of soul stealing are the source of what new-age culture calls 'channelling'. (Many people think channelling is a good thing, but, for every channeller who becomes rich and famous, there are many others who uncontrollably channel pure drivel, or worse, destructive impulses.) Soul stealing, at its most severe, is one of the features of schizophrenia. Here the mechanism that suppresses the voices in an average adult is also affected and the condition is out of control.

I quote Grant again:

"The good news is that soul pieces don't have us, we have them! Contrary to what the movies or most healers say about this, no matter how bad it is, even if it drives us crazy or causes us to harm other people, we're hanging on to them, they're not hanging on to us "

The soul pieces that most people feel are in the form of voices, but some are tactile: they make you feel like someone else. It depends which part of your body you've stored the piece in. They can also be emotions, if they are stored in your heart area; they will manifest as an emotion that comes up each time a certain trigger is activated, an emotion that doesn't seem to belong to you. In my example below, I suspect that the feeling of being old and undesirable actually belonged to the person I swiped all those soul pieces from. It was unshakeable while I had the soul pieces, but it was an uncharacteristic emotion for me and it vanished when I healed the last piece. (By contrast, 'copied' emotions are rarely so disruptive in the present.)

To heal soul stealing, use the simplest form of what we call the Silent Mind Technique:

1) Find the emotional tone of the intruding voice, emotion or sensation.

2) Imagine yourself in a bubble, and the bubble is holding the emotion, or saying the phrase of the soul piece. Be completely surrounded by this sensation or feeling-tone or phrase, as if it were your mother's womb and you were inside it.

3) Move your attention into your lower belly.

4) From the perspective of your belly, love yourself for surviving, for hanging on to this sensation in order to survive.
   (More specifically, if your perceptions are detailed enough, love yourself as the contact point between the 'holding on to this' and the 'surviving'. This is how Grant teaches it, but until recently I didn't understand what this meant. My sensations had never been fine-tuned enough to tell this small aspect apart from the whole problem. A few days ago, however, I finally experienced, in the context of a different kind of injury, what he meant. He would say: "Love is the solvent between this sensation of holding on and this other sensation of wanting so much to survive." This might speed things up. If you can't do it, the process will still work.)

The soul piece often releases suddenly, with the sensation of something whooshing away or a sudden, tiny memory loss: "Who was this person again?"

At other times, the healing takes longer: once you've done the above, a more involved trauma might appear. Heal it like any other trauma, making sure you identify the physical component of the injury. The example below describes one of each of those situations, the simple and the complex.

The problem of soul stealing is one of the reasons why it's dangerous to merge consciousnesses with someone else. Our advanced training teaches how to eliminate this problem. *Until you take this training, please consider it dangerous to merge with anyone who is alive in the present.* In later sections, you will be instructed to merge with different images that appear around you while you regress. This is intrinsically safe, *as long as you do not merge with people who are alive in the present.* The only exceptions are your parents and your grandparents, and even there, it is only safe to merge consciousnesses with them from the point of view of a prenatal trauma, from a regressed state.

The following example is also from my notebooks. I'd been the first guinea pig for a generic Silent Mind process (the process that eliminates our drive to grab soul pieces in the first place, as opposed to the one above, that eliminates soul pieces one by one). Everyone thought I had healed the whole thing, but as it turned out, I had only done half. Meanwhile I had a session with a client I'll call Marian. I practised my new merging skills on her. I'd experimented with merging before, with several people, and with no ill effects. But this time was different.

> Since the session with Marian, which did go all right, I feel out of sorts... Ashamed of myself, as I used to feel after speaking in public or teaching. Plus I feel old, finished, undesirable. But also, I feel... like Marian. Tactilely, physically like her, I mean. That part is quite pleasant, really: I feel that little corner of a smile she has, and the way she holds her head proud, her tallness and her grace. It's quite uncanny. And it's lasted beyond the usual 2 or 3 minutes of vividly feeling like the person I've merged with. It's been hours.
>
> It's soul stealing, of course. Oops. And I thought I was safe...
>
> Phoned Grant. He guided me to make a surrounding bubble out of the Marian-ness, and feel from my lower belly. Love myself for surviving and for holding on. It seemed good at first: after about 20 minutes, I suddenly had a blank: "What was her name again? How weird, I can't remember." The soul piece had gone. Yeah, yeah: people usually do this in a minute or so, but for me, 20 minutes is not bad. But then the Marian-ness returned. With another emotional tone, so it's a different soul piece. Great, how many did I take on?

The answer was: many. Seven or eight. It took a while to get rid of them. The traumas were severe and earlier than we'd thought possible for soul stealing. I'll spare you the middle part; here's the end.

Next session:

I surround myself with this new emotional tone. That feeling of being old, undesirable.

My body is like a small nave, a container. Solar plexus holds the beginnings of a disgust for myself, which I know to be profound. I love myself with my disgust. As soon as this is healed, I return to my body consciousness, feeling from my belly, vessel-like.

My world is dying. Loving myself in a dying world.

Maybe Père is smoking? He used to, long ago, didn't he? My dying world, so far from its purpose.

Weird: I'm glad that, although Grant's father died, Grant himself is still alive -- wait, this isn't exactly a distraction: I suddenly get brighter.

Now I get it: that seemingly idle thought signalled a belief starting to move: the belief that we are forever tied to our fathers' fate, emotions, life and death. I just love myself with the remainder of that belief.

It's as if a pile of Père's oppressed state suddenly had cleared out! Not quite a 'whoosh' feeling, but almost. Certainly something has gone. It's as if he suddenly wasn't there anymore.

This was indeed the last of those soul pieces. Several of them moved off at that moment. It also clearly showed as a sperm trauma, confirming the key to complete the Silent Mind process (we had previously thought it was only an egg problem). Marian's feeling-tones had been similar to my father's at those early moments. The feelings associated with the soul pieces never reappeared. And I became a staunch advocate for caution in the use of merging, because I know how miserable those soul pieces can make one feel.

Soul Loss

Soul loss happens when a chunk of your own 'soul' (see previous section) has been ejected during an extremely severe trauma.

Rarely, at the end of a session, you might feel a sensation of loss or lack or flatness centred in your chest. The feeling will disappear spontaneously in a few hours or days, but you can resolve the problem instantly by singing the very first melody that pops into your mind. The lack vanishes quickly - within seconds, or at most a few minutes. [20]

Sometimes the lack is so severe that one simply can't get enough breath to sing aloud! (I'm the only person I know of who has experienced this.) If this should happen, heal whatever feelings arise while you try to sing. Keep trying, and heal whatever feelings come up with that choking breath. The lack will eventually vanish.

Pretend-Identities

Notwithstanding all the above cautions about merging, this is where I'll start telling you to merge with everything you see. But we're not dealing with your live contemporaries here: we're talking about all the stray bits of your subconscious that need reclaiming, in the context of a regressed state.

Pretend-identities (also called self-identities or self-images in Grant's writings) are exactly what they sound like. One of your triune brains, under severe stress, has decided, "I'm not really here, this isn't really me."

The most common pretend-identities are the ones assumed by the egg and sperm. The egg feels like your mother. Then it feels like every woman you've ever known. The sperm feels like your father. Then it feels like every guy you've ever met. It's a handy way to say, this isn't my problem, it's my mother's fault, it's my father's fault, all women are the same, all men are that way. For goodness' sake, let's blame someone else.

We're so creative. Any brain, at any time, can decide to pretend it's something else than a frightened little component of you. It will grab images from mythology, symbols from womb development or early life, or characters from the movie you saw yesterday.

Pretend-identities are hard to imagine until you encounter one in healing. Then they're obvious. You find yourself in disguise: looking and feeling like one of your parents, or, more strangely, a lizard, say, or an

---

[20] Another example of how incomplete our knowledge is at times... Tal noted that she often encounters soul loss at the outset of a session: "People come in with a sense of loss, missing something, lack, not being whole." Grant has mostly seen it at the end. Tal also mentions soul loss in various locations in the body. It's possible that we have more than one phenomenon here. With a sense of lack at the outset of a session, I would try the treatment for "Emptiness", to see if any emotion is hiding inside the lack. Tal has unusual perceptions and can discriminate between soul loss and emptiness, but most of us can't. Emptiness is much more common, so, when in doubt, that's where I would put my wager.

evil monster, or your grandmother, or an ugly bug, or just about anything. I remember two sessions in a row where my solar plexus felt like a big furry spider. Its belief was that it was so loathsome that everyone, including the rest of me, should run away in fear.

Healing pretend-identities is straightforward: where is this sensation? Stay in your body, in the part of your body that feels disguised. If the pretend-identity seems to be apart from you, merge with it: put it on like a sweater. Love yourself as you are; you haven't changed that much, you're just frightened. Be whatever you are in this moment until the hidden emotion and body sensation arise. Then continue with the basic method.

Archetypal Images

> *"Joseph Campbell (...) stated that all archetypes and patternings of the deep psyche are, in effect, only the organs of the body interacting with each other"*[21]

I lump into this category any part of you that seems to be outside your body in the past. Under the heading 'Projections', I'll discuss the projecting of past traumas onto something or someone outside you *in the present.*

Archetypal images are very similar to pretend-identities, but they seem much more intimidating because they appear to be separate from you. They occur for the same reasons as pretend-identities and projections. In fact, they *are* projections; but since we heal them a bit differently from the usual kind of projection, I will discuss them separately.

To understand archetypal images, it's essential to remember the triune nature of the brain. Our brains are supposed to function in such harmony that they are fused and undistinguishable from each other, but, for the majority of us, conflicts are the norm. More: most of us treat at least one of our brains as a complete stranger. In our culture, the body brain is the one most commonly cast aside, although a significant number of people have trouble accessing their heart.

When we start healing ourselves, our resistance to feeling all of our brains starts to ebb. And often the first impression of the separated brain

---

[21] W. Brugh Joy, *Avalanche*, p.40. The statement came from a video series Campbell did with Bill Moyers.

is as an outside, threatening image. Most people's first vision of their body brain is as some variation of the monster in the basement. Mine looked like a swamp monster. Drippy, gooey, making wet slurpy sounds. Very convincing. The image or impression is often incredibly vivid. To compound the problem, our body is the most powerful of the brains, and the other brains can feel so threatened by it that they will make up an image that is either terrifyingly evil or forbiddingly god-like.

W. Brugh Joy, in his book *Avalanche*, unwittingly gives us a magnificent example of the body brain awakening as the image of evil. Dr. Joy had been living in some type of mind-heart fusion, a peak state he called 'the heart chakra state of consciousness'.[22] Predictably, after a few years, his body brain decided that it should be safe to come out and play. Its first manifestation was in a nightmare: Dr. Joy dreamed of stopping for gas on the highway and meeting a gang of evil-looking bikers. He tries to make his escape, locks himself in his car and guns it out of there just in the nick of time... only to find that Evil Incarnate is now sitting in the back seat.

Ah, the Evil in the back seat... The monster in the basement... Good ol' body brain. Unfortunately, Dr. Joy didn't have the data to solve that one, so instead of just merging with Evil Incarnate and welcoming his poor body home, he proceeded to write a 300-page rationalization for the evil in us.

Body Brain doesn't have the monopoly on archetypal images. Here's a more pedestrian example from a recent session with a student I'll call Edith. The renegade, in this case, is one aspect of her mind brain:

> Trigger is betrayal. It scores an eight out of ten on the distress scale.
>
> Edith can think of several instances of betrayal... She goes to the earliest: her father is beating her up. She's very young.
>
> "I see a yellow monster," she says, delineating with her hands a large area to the right of her head. I instruct her to merge with that yellow monster: bring it to herself, put it on like a sweater, look out of its eyes and become it as much as possible. "Now scan for new feelings or body sensations."
>
> "It feels like... justification. In my throat."
>
> She does the usual drill: stays with the justification in her throat, loves herself for trying to justify herself.
>
> "It feels yellow."
>
> "Well... love yourself for feeling yellow!"
>
> "Now it's peaceful."

---

[22] Possibly the Beauty Way, by our Institute's nomenclature; it may have been combined with a fully blossoming heart chakra.

Did I mention that Edith is one of the fastest healers I've ever seen? This took five minutes and took her sense of betrayal to 2 out of 10. She healed one more injury — a generational trauma, no less — and took it to zero. Total time elapsed: fifteen minutes. Did I also mention it was her first session?

We find all sorts of things outside our bodies during sessions.[23] Again, as long as it's not someone who is alive in the present, it's safe to merge with whatever it is, no matter how awful it looks. You might see the goddess Diana, an Aztec god who rips out hearts, an immense standing stone, angels, spirits, demons, a vision of Jesus Christ on the cross… It's all safe. It's you. It's an unclaimed part of you. Merge with it, love yourself as *it*, look for new sensations and emotions in your body, and heal everything you find. I will again emphasize that even evil is safe to merge with. The feeling of evil is an emotion, just like any other emotion. In all the years of exploring, not one of our crew has ever encountered a real Satan. You might find a place that looks like hell, and see something that looks like the embodiment of evil, but if you merge with it and sit there just accepting, with no agenda to change anything, eventually it heals. Evil in us is, at root, a very human misunderstanding.

Here's another session from a student I'll call Ludovic. First session, too. The 'shadows leaving' halfway through the session were almost certainly soul pieces. I'm intrigued by the 'swirling' he felt around him. It sometimes is the first sign of a vortex (see that section below), but in this case it seemed to contain the soul pieces. I don't know what the other things around his head were. I don't know what moment he regressed to. The horizon line suggests something very early, precellular (during the formation of the egg or sperm). It would be nice to know all that, but it's not necessary. The healing works regardless.

Ludovic saw two archetypal images at the same time. The gambit of merging with both at once did work. If, for some reason, it hadn't, we could have dealt with each in turn.

> Trigger: feeling of being pressured, uncertainty.
>
> Swirling around him. Loves himself with the swirling, pressure and uncertainty.
>
> Gone? Yes, gone already. He feels 'happiness'.

---

[23] The example of my first experience of my own placenta as a threatening attacker, described at the beginning of this chapter, is another case in point.

Re-triggers himself by re-reading the words he wrote to describe the problem at the session's start. Frustration in his head. Swirling sensation is still present.

"I see the kind of black I would see with my eyes closed in the dark: stove black, with waves. A mouth shouting. A scorpion."

He merges into the mouth and the scorpion, becomes both simultaneously. New sensation: tightness in spine. Confusion. Loves himself as all that.

Shadows leaving him! Two?

"Are there still shapes out there, around you?"

"Yes, around my head. I see one, a bright one."

He merged with it, healed the sensations; it became integrated. More small things around his head. Took one in: sensation of split vision. Loved himself with the discomfort of that. It became a horizon line, and the feeling was joy.

More shapes around his head. "Many, like rain." I had him widen to take in all the rain, become all of it, and in a very short time he felt... forgiveness.

No sense of anything around him anymore. Calm, peaceful, light.

Generational Traumas

Some traumas pass down from generation to generation. Think about addiction problems, patterns of violence in a family, a propensity for certain diseases, but also more subtle things like shyness, phobias, certain beliefs about the world.

Generational traumas are high on the list of causes for a stuck healing. The healing goes nowhere; what's worse, the trauma feels really, really personal, as if it were about the present, about how you are and will be forever, not about a moment from years and years ago when you were a tiny fetus in a womb. Generational traumas tend to 'stick' if you interrupt a session. You end up dragging the traumatic feelings around with you instead of returning fully in the present. Even worse: sometimes the generational string hides at the bottom of a hole... Double trouble.

I generally try to run away from healing generational stuff, to convince myself I'm imagining things. It never works... I always end up having to face the damn things before I can go on. And I'm always glad I did. The task, before I tackle it, always seems far more difficult than it really is.

Whenever you suspect a generational trauma, look or feel around for a sensation of people nearby while you're in regression. Check again: is there only one person, a sequential row of them, or a group of contemporaries, like a tribe?

Often we see one person to begin with, but then get the sensation of a row or string of people, or a deck or cards with one person on each card. The pattern usually runs diagonally away from our body. This is the most commonly seen pattern, especially with people new to regression healing. Heal this by merging with the ancestor who's furthest away from you. This will be the earliest, the first generation that developed the pattern. Stay in your own body, and bring the image of this ancestor to you — even if you only have a vague sense of a blob of light or 'something out there'. Yes, faking it does work. Become this person: your mind is his mind, your heart is his heart, your belly is his belly. Love yourself as this person. Details will start to emerge. Don't worry if you don't get a full bio. It might be more like, "I think I'm male... standing atop a cliff, maybe? Don't see anything, just an impression of wind on grass... Like a seaside cliff maybe. It's lonely here." Again, the pedigree of this person does not matter. What matters, as usual, is, how do you feel as this person? What are the emotions, the body sensations? Heal these just as you would heal them in yourself. It's probably a relief because, even if the emotions are very intense, they no longer feel so personal.

How long should you stay merged, how completely should you heal this person? This is open for debate. At minimum, stay until the presenting trauma, the one you first noticed when you merged with this ancestor, has gone away and there's at least temporary calm, peace and lightness. Better: if you have the patience and the ancestor isn't absolutely loaded with damage, heal him or her completely *in the moment when you merged with him or her* (there's no need to go exploring the rest of this person's life; just stay in the one moment, otherwise it could take you ages to heal everything!). The ancestor often dissolves in light or walks away peacefully at this point. Best: at least three Institute researchers have found, independently of each other, that when an ancestor seems fully healed but is still visible, staying merged and in a state of acceptance for a few minutes more sometimes allows you to receive the *positive* inheritance from that person. Traumas aren't the only things that can be passed on! What I've 'received' are mostly insights and teachings of a spiritual nature. Usually they're impossible to explain to anyone, but it's always a comforting experience, and occasionally the insights have been very useful.

Some people will access generational traumas by asking themselves, about the stuck emotion, "Who felt like this? My mother or my father? -

and merging with that trauma moment in the parent that feels like the right one... then asking again, as that parent, "Who felt like this? My mother or father?" - and so on, one generation at a time, until they cannot find anything earlier.[24]

Here's an example of a student I'll call Ariane, in her second session, healing a generational line and experiencing the positive counterpart of the trauma. Notice the mix of accurate factual images (her birth parents, her placenta *in utero*) and metaphors (toxins seen as rusty screws and tin cans in her bloodstream). This is a regular and captivating feature of this healing modality. We tend to see metaphors of whatever images seem too threatening or far-fetched. With experience, people see more and more of the literal, biological events during their regressions. Indeed, it's quite possible that the ancestral images are wholesale metaphors as well, standing in for genetic damage[25] - which would help explain why it is safe to merge with these images of long-ago people, seen in regression, and not with people in the present. But there's often a wealth of historical details, and some therapists have been able to verify the accuracy of their clients' ancestral regressions.

> Trigger: anxiety about having to move to a new house. She remembers the same feeling when she had to move at the onset of her puberty. Then she sees an image of her birth parents arguing about her. (Ariane was adopted.) Then something even earlier with the same feeling-tone: toxic stuff surrounding her *in utero* - so she's moved backwards in time, from a background of toxic emotions to literally toxic surroundings.
>
> Trauma seems to be in the area immediately around her. It's probably her placenta, so I instruct her to widen her awareness to take it all in. Sure enough, her placenta is trying to protect her body. The toxic stuff feels like tin cans and rusty screws! And the injury feels very personal. I instruct her to again pay attention to her surroundings.
>
> It seems at first like a circle of people around her, holding hands. When I ask her to guess at whether they're contemporaries of each other or a generational line, the image resolves itself as a wide spiral of people, with her

---

[24] This isn't a fool-proof method. One time, I tried it while an advanced healer, who had already spotted the trauma, looked on; I got it exactly wrong.

[25] Or rather, epigenetic damage: experiments with advanced healing techniques show that many traumas track back to damage to the genes' coatings or surroundings, not to the genes themselves. The images of ancestors, then, would be a sort of memory imprinted in the genes or in their immediate surroundings, and our regression a travel inwards through these imprinted memories, rather than outside our bodies and to ancient times.

at the centre. I ask her to merge into the ancestor who's right at the other end of the line. At first, this ancestor just feels like a vague ball of light.

Ariane merges into the ball of light. I instruct her to love herself as this ancestor, and heal her just as she would heal herself: Where is the injury? What's the emotion?

"It looks like this woman took some poison, she thought this stuff she took would make her powerful."

After just a few minutes, the ancestor feels calm, peaceful and bright. I invite Ariane to stay merged for a few more minutes and see if any further changes happen.

"...It's like a cleansing ceremony... I'm the one being cleansed! I'm in the middle of a sacred circle, and I'm a unicorn." Ariane remained until she felt a sense of completion, gave her thanks to the ancestor, and returned to her own body (simply by reorienting herself in her body, in the present).

There was still a sense of toxicity in her placenta, but it didn't feel personal anymore, and the rest of the injury released easily. Ariane finished with a sense of clarity. "It feels like I have a better sense of boundaries."

"And how do you feel about moving, now?"

"It doesn't matter; my body is my home."

If you see a group of people and they seem to be contemporaries of each other, not a generational line, you're probably at the bottom of a vortex. (Yes, it's entirely possible to end up there without ever experiencing any spinning.) See next section.

Whenever you finish healing a generational trauma, check yourself for any remaining injury on the same theme. As you saw in the example above, the remaining traumas only hold minimal emotional charge and usually resolve quickly. If they do not, look for a further generational line.

Vortices

Grant insists that vortices are not generational traumas, even if they make you encounter events that seem to have happened to ancestors. My own theory is that both generational traumas and vortices cause us to access genetic material; vortices give us access to mitochondrial DNA, which is separate from, and feels much older than, the rest of your DNA, probably because it is indeed much older.

But that's my own opinion, formed during my own sessions, so let's be conciliatory here and say that vortices not generational traumas, but they sure are weird. They may have the same emotional overtones as the generational lines we saw in the previous section, but the initial sensations are different, the root cause is different, and they're handled a bit differently. Sometimes the first clue is a sense of dizziness. It may be a dizziness you've felt so often, you'll tend to dismiss it. Some people initially describe it as confusion or vertigo. As you focus your attention into the sensation, you might feel yourself spinning; or you might visually perceive a tornado somewhere in your body.

Abandon yourself completely to the movement: put yourself inside the tornado. Slowly make your way down towards the narrow end, feeling and accepting any traumatic sensations on the way. (It's the same general idea as healing a hole, except you keep traveling down instead of exploring around and around.) The tornado sensation might last several minutes and be anywhere from slight to the wildest circus ride.

Sink into that spinning until you can sink no more and the movement stops. You're likely to sense a group of people, often feeling like 'ancient ones', at that point (some people just perceive a collective of vague oval shapes; this is actually closer to what's happening at the cellular level. More rarely it looks like a group tableau from your own life; on one occasion I saw just one individual). Merge with the group: just take them all in. Love yourself as the whole group; the key technique here is to really, really honour everything these people are feeling, everything they're going through.[26]

There's usually a central figure who seems more significant and on whom you can focus, but do keep the whole group in your perception. Again, this is easier done than said. Emotions and physical sensations will surface in definite locations in your body. Heal whatever you find until the whole group disappears or becomes a cloud of brightness.

---

[26] Speaking of honouring: I'd like to honour here the healer Maureen Chandler, who first identified vortices as structures containing traumas. Maureen discovered that vortices are sometimes associated with addictions. A Crosby vortex is a vortex that contributes to an addiction. Maureen named this phenomenon in remembrance of her father.

A footnote to the footnote: our study of addictions is still in its infancy. Our early results suggest that addictions often hide extremely severe traumas, and these traumas, in turn, often block access to very powerful changes of consciousness. Healing can sometimes spark serious disruptions. I strongly recommend that you seek qualified supervision if you plan to heal an addiction. This said, 'dry' addictions (leftover cravings after quitting the addictive substance for a long period) seem to be more straightforward to heal. But please do get help anyway.

Occasionally there are two ringleaders to heal. Tal gives an example that clarifies the ringleader concept. She writes:

> If you heal the leader, the whole group dissolves. If you miss the leader, keep trying until you find him. The leader may be hiding, or may not be the strongest in the picture. One student saw a group of people enslaved, and merged with the man with the whip. Healing him did not help, but then looking again, he found that one of the slaves, though weak in body and not large, seems to be a father figure to the rest. Healing him fixed the vortex.

I've had success healing groups as a whole without the perception of a leader, too. Here's such an example: one of the first groups I healed. It was part of a series of healings with end-of-the-world overtones. Some very early moments of our consciousness often feel that way, like the creation or destruction of a world. This is one example of ending up with the group of ancestors without ever perceiving a vortex. No problem: it's the ancestors, or whatever genetic or epigenetic damage they stand for, who hold the key to the trauma.

> ...I see myself as a set of short vertical tubes at the edge of a grey fog. A sense of dread about the future. Or I'm a group of prehistoric people at the edge of primordial ice.
>
> Lots of anger in each brain. It seems endless. It's going nowhere. I persist in calling the image of the group at the edge of the ice 'mythical': a metaphor, an alternate view of those tubes at the edge of the mist. And it stays right in my face, unchanged. So I finally quit procrastinating and read it as ancestral: a vortex without the spinning. I merge into the collectivity of them.
>
> Instant deluge of emotions! Misery, cold, fear, anger at life. Heavy sense of responsibility for the family. All this centred in my solar plexus. Feels like a family grouping, lost, maybe on the Bering ice bridge? Something very old, at any rate.
>
> After a while, I start feeling some life around us: fish and sea mammals under the ice. Maybe a bird or two. I'm still not crazy about this situation, but it's not quite as hopeless anymore. Maybe we'll survive.
>
> Then peace. The group seems to vanish in the mist, and I move to my own trauma, more aspects of the problem of responsibility, still in my solar plexus. Then suddenly I glimpse the family on the ice again, and I laugh and laugh: it now looks like they're on a bloody picnic outing! Life teems around them: birds, fish and sea mammals. They've reconnected to their environment and know its nurturing abundance.
>
> I solve more of the related fears in myself. Then move on to an earlier trauma...

Now here's an example of a full-blown vortex. I was experimenting with regression to very early events. Note also the projection of an aspect of my trauma on my teacher. This is a very, very common dynamic.

> This time it's more a dizziness, a sense of falling. I abandon myself to the movement and the next thing, after I heal a trauma or two having to do with that sense of falling, initially looks like thoughts about people, or it looks like people as a metaphor for my own emotions, but come to think of it they *are* people, vaguely familiar, in a landscape.
>
> I merge with them.
>
> They seem to be hanging on to some internal light, maybe a metaphor for spiritual progress? The holding on is terribly, physically painful, and there's a sense of being in limbo. Then they let go to some degree and are less bright but the suffering lessens.
>
> Loss, loss: hearts clinging to a ball of light as it exits...
>
> "It's all I have!" (Attachment to their/my spiritual growth so far.)
>
> I think of my teacher, who sounded yesterday like I'm nothing but genes, nothing but physical stuff, at this early stage of development... my own belief that I'm something more, something spiritual. A feeling of being denied my humanity, in the form of that light...
>
> Then suddenly it resolves: the ancestors are dynamic, bright moving balls of light. There is no stasis, no possible way to stop and hoard your progress once you start on this road. We are dynamic entities.

Not everything that spins is a vortex; vertigo doesn't always take you down a tornado. Sometimes, in regression, we experience chakras; they spin slower than vortices and feel somewhat ornamental -- and sometimes they are injured. Movement in the amniotic fluid also may feel dizzying. Abandon yourself to whatever movement you feel, welcoming the sensations. Heal whatever you find. There is no right and wrong here, just exploration and acceptance.

Past Lives

Ah: a nicely controversial subject. I started this work disbelieving that past lives existed, and, despite thousands of hours spent in regression, I'm still not sure where I stand on the subject.

Again, I prefer focusing on the experiential aspect and leaving the philosophical debates to others. Are past lives literal truths, metaphors for something we can't encompass, absolute delusions? It doesn't matter to the work of healing yourself. What does matter is believing that the images we encounter in regression are *something*, whether it's literal or symbolic; dealing with the images, as we encounter them, with love and acceptance; and getting the desired result, which is not the validation of this or that philosophical position but the permanent resolution of traumas.

People *do* encounter, in regression, images that look like past lives. You can tell a past life apart from a generational trauma because the past-life person really feels like you. You, but transformed: you in period clothing with maybe a gender swap and a cultural change, but definitely *you*. Sometimes you recognize other people from your present lifetime nearby.

For example, once, out of the blue, I found myself transplanted from a womb moment to laying face down on the ground inside a tepee. Impression of scars on my shoulders, exhaustion, sense of failure. It really felt like *me,* being a Plains Indian having messed up his (or her, I couldn't tell) Sundance ceremony. There was no sense of this being my ancestor. Okay, and at that point I still don't believe in past lives, so what am I doing here?

This is where I was grateful for those who had blazed the healing trail before me: I had already learned that past lives are nearly always red herrings.

I'll let Grant do the talking again, from *The Basic Whole-Hearted Healing Manual:*

> "One of the more controversial discoveries that we've made in the last few years is that encountering a past life memory is *not* the core of the issue. Clients access past-life material to escape a similar sensation in this lifetime. You can choose to heal the past-life memory or not, but once the pressure is handled from the past life, perhaps for practice, the trauma in this lifetime needs to be healed.
>
> "For the typical person, there are so many lifetimes that trying to heal them all is completely pointless. We access those moments simply because those particular past-life traumas have a similar sensation to the ones in this lifetime." [27]

---

[27] *The Basic Whole-Hearted Healing Manual,* p. 55. But Grant added this as a recent comment to this manuscript: " I'm a bit undecided on this now. To be safe, I actually heal the past life and the present life if there is time, just in case. Perhaps the past life stimulated the present life trauma?" ...Oh boy. More uncertainty. I told you we didn't agree on everything! See also footnote 29.

I have enough traumas of my own, thank you, and I've always decided against trying to heal past-life images 'for practice'. I treat them as attempts to evade the core issue, love myself for doing this, and return to my own sensations in my own body in my own lifetime.

But what about the people who heal 'karmic issues' through past-life regression? I can't claim to know much about past-life regression techniques. (Do people end up with solid, permanent changes, or merely with a good intellectual reframing of their problem?) But, reading through case histories, I'm discovering that some confusion exists on what actually constitutes a past-life experience.

Consider this example from Stanislav Grof's *The Cosmic Game.*[28] In a section titled *Verification of Past Life Memories,* Grof reports the experience of a woman doing regression therapy and experiencing herself as a 17th-century Czech nobleman who gets executed, with others, in Prague's public square. "In this case, the patient's father conducted, unbeknownst to her, independent genealogical research of the family's pedigree, which confirmed that they were descendants of one of these unfortunate men."

Grof categorizes this experience as a 'verified past life'. But it's not a past life; it's a generational trauma. This makes me wonder how many 'past-life experiences' that resulted in real changes to the clients' lives are, in fact, generational. To add yet more confusion, some generational traumas are *also* past lives. (You feel like yourself but you also sense with clarity that you are, for example, your own great-great-grandmother...) If it has a generational component, heal it. Otherwise, unless you are curious, or more cautious than I am, or need the practice, return to your own body sensations in your current life.

If you do choose to heal a past life, do it the same way you would heal the present one. Be in your body as the past-life person, feel the emotions and body sensations, love yourself with no agenda but acceptance. *Do not* attempt to change your past life from the standpoint of your 'greater experience' in the present. Such attempts are usually misguided. The healing that occurs from simply staying in your body and loving yourself is in alignment with what's best for that person at that time. Love and accept yourself as you are and see what changes occur.

I only once felt the need to heal a past-life segment. It looked like the death of whoever I seemed to be in the life immediately preceding my present one. The feelings of anger, fear and loss seemed to impinge on

---

[28] *The Cosmic Game*, p. 168.

the very first moments of my consciousness in my present life. I was working with an advanced healer and we decided to experiment with healing the very last moment of this other person's life. It did seem to free up the current-life trauma. Was it necessary? I may never know.[29]

More food for thought: Grof, again,[30] notes that people's perceptions of and opinions about past lives change with their state of consciousness.

> "A typical member of the western industrial civilization believes that he or she is a physical body. This clearly limits existence to a life span that reaches from conception to the moment of death. (...)
>
> "[In a better state of consciousness] we think about ourselves as open-ended chains of lifetimes, and see our karmic partners in the same way.
>
> "If we continue our inner journey, additional holotropic experiences can show us that even spatial boundaries are ultimately illusory and can be dissolved. (...) At this point, we identify with the unified field of cosmic creative energy and with Absolute Consciousness. From this perspective, the past life dramas represent just another level of illusion (...). We do not believe in karma anymore, certainly not in the same sense we did before."

The latter - minus the lofty subtext - best describes my own position. Indeed, my perceptions and beliefs have shifted so much through this work that I don't necessarily see time as linear anymore. The impression is that all our lives, past, present and future, are somehow occurring simultaneously. In this context, it seems much more useful to focus on the life I'm living right now. All these selves, if they are not illusions, are working at versions of the same problem.

---

[29] Recently, Tal documented a stronger connection than we'd suspected between a past-life trauma and present-day damage. Once again, this was an instance of the ending of a recent life. In this light, I'd say that if the trauma seems to 'stick' and fails to heal after you've decided to skip a past-life memory, it could indicate a need to return to it. If the past-life person dies, stay until all life is gone and everything is peaceful.

Tal writes, "Heal a past life if it is directly affecting your present life. You know that this is the case if the first place you reach in regression is the past life. That time I healed the past life back in Canada, the trauma was like a huge hole in my chest, and I was in mortal fear." She also wrote about her connections to past-life experiences in general: "When I meet a past life and merge with it, there is a little piece of me that clicks with a little piece of them. This feels like my true self - beyond traumas and cultures and any of the overlaying junk. It gives amazing insight. "

[30] Op. cit., p. 182.

Projections

Suppose you are convinced that the issue belongs to someone else. You, yourself, are fine; the problem is that your partner has power issues, your neighbour is a drama queen, your kids keep lying to you, your boss is evil. And *that* is really bugging you.

Please be willing to set aside that certainty. We do a lot more projection than we think. Whenever a trauma is too uncomfortable, we try very hard to make it look like it's someone else's problem. If I have anger that I don't want to acknowledge, for example, I'm likely to see anger everywhere I look — other people's anger. Or so I think. More: when a trauma gets stimulated and we refuse to own it, we actually put out an unspoken request for other people to act in a certain way. The people most likely to pick up and honour those requests are our nearest and dearest: spouses, parents, children, and — once we start learning to heal ourselves — our mentors and teachers.

If we eliminate the projection, these people change the way they act with us. They might still interact the same way with other people, but at least it doesn't affect us anymore.

Does this mean that you should blame and hate yourself every time someone bothers you? Not in the least. Recall our discussion about the triune brains: projections are about the feelings held by parts of your awareness to which you have no conscious access at the moment. Compassion, towards yourself and the person acting out, is a much more appropriate and productive response.

Suspect a projection anytime someone's behaviour disturbs you. If there is no projection, the other person might do profoundly stupid things *but you are calm, peaceful and light about it.* Suspect a projection, especially, anytime you find yourself running into the same sort of annoyances repeatedly (for example, you keep meeting control freaks or drama queens or procrastinators).

We once even saw a case of stalking that turned out to be a powerful projection. The victim, during a healing session, tried 'owning' the qualities she saw in this man who kept following her home and making odd phone calls. She realized, to her astonishment, that *her* body brain was attracted to *him*! His behaviour ceased immediately, without the need for confrontation.

We project onto people, and we project onto objects. Remember my relative, the restaurant owner, whose appliances kept breaking down? That was almost certainly an instance of projection. Another example:

one of my Institute colleagues had been running into a series of technical glitches, and I challenged him to look for the projections in them, just to see how far we could push this idea. One day, his car's automatic lock system malfunctioned. The keys were in the car... He hadn't locked himself out; the car had locked *him* out. When he regressed on the associated emotions, he found himself in a conception moment. His car represented the egg, asking, "*And who is this you're letting in?*" A few weeks later, a virus shut down his computer. All his programs were useless. He did another healing session, loving himself as the equivalent of the useless, incapacitated machine. No kidding: after the session, he turned his computer on, and it had regained about 80% of its function. (We're joking about starting a new business: Inner Peace Computers. 'Never mind the machine, leave it at home: we work on the owner.')

My latest one is not so drastic, but closer to the usual resolution of a projection on an object.

> My roof had been leaking for months, and I'd tried patching it with tar, to no avail, then had the hardest time finding a roofer, and then his waiting list was months long; and *then* the wettest winter on record started. I tried and tried healing it as a projection, feeling the drips as tears, healing sadness, while I also got on the phone trying to solve things, and on the roof adding tarps. One day I listened to yet another drip, falling softly on the new bathroom floor. Fear. It sounds like... no, not tears. Blood. Blood dripping. I focus on that. The fear is outside me, on the periphery. Placenta, then. I widen my awareness to include it. It's birth: my cord is cut; blood is dripping onto a metal hospital table... that soft, sad sound.
>
> I healed everything in sight. Not a huge sense of resolution, and the roof still drips... but when it does, the water falls directly into the bathroom sink! The roofing materials showed up this morning, I've met the repair crew and they're nice, capable people. It all seems effortless now, instead of overwhelming.

Essentially, we heal projections in the same way as we heal other images that seem to be outside us, with one very important difference: as I noted in the section on soul stealing, *it is unsafe, for someone in average consciousness, to merge with a person who is alive in the present.* So we take a detour and transfer the qualities onto a neutral object, then merge with that.

Exercise: Healing a projection

1) Think about someone whose behaviour has been a problem for you lately. (Yes, it could be an animal or a thing as well. In one of our first experiments with this technique, one student chose the entire city of Chicago.)

Note that the projection could be a set of positive qualities. (For example: "my sister is so unattainably good and wonderful and how can I ever hope to be anything like her?")

2) Write down how you feel about this person. Go wild. This isn't the time for political correctness or "I" statements. Lay it on with a spatula. Get it out of your system. (If the projection appears in the middle of a session, just do this step mentally, because writing stuff down is too likely to pull you out of the regression.) If you're dealing with a series of projections, treat all the misbehaving people—all the procrastinators or control freaks and so on—as one person.

3) If your feelings *about* the projection are overwhelming, heal them now before proceeding to the next step. If it still looks like the other party is the one with the main problem, skip this step and go to step 4.

4) Imagine a voodoo doll, or a stick figure, or just a generic grey blob (one therapist I know uses an actual teddy bear!). Now imagine that you're pasting all those annoying characteristics onto this thing, making a three-dimensional figure that contains the characteristics of the person who's bugging you.

5) Merge with the figure! (*NOT with the annoying person him- or herself! Because, one, you're* not *trying to heal him or her; and two, you must protect yourself from swiping soul pieces.*) If there's a lot of resistance to merging, don't worry—it's normal; this is why you projected the trauma in the first place! Just heal your resistance, (as in step 3) and then try again.

6) Scan your body for new or exacerbated emotions or physical sensations. If there's a new or renewed emotion, where is it located? If it's a body sensation, what is the emotion inside it? Note that the feeling inside a projection does not necessarily match its outside appearance. Just accept whatever is there. Welcome it home: it's you.

7) Heal the emotions and physical sensations the usual way. Keep going until you're calm, peaceful and lightweight.

8) Check your work: think about this troublesome person again. You won't necessarily feel an overwhelming love for him, but you should feel calm, peaceful and light about what he's been doing. If you don't, repeat the exercise for any remaining aspects.

9) In the days following the exercise, note any change in this person's behaviour.

Note that this does not heal *all* your projections on this particular person once and for all. It's still possible that you will later project other, different traumas onto this same person. Again, family members are our very favourite mirrors. But if you completely healed the trauma, this particular problem should be completely and permanently gone.

Here are some examples of healing following this method. The first one occurred in a student's first session with me—her third regression experience in all. 'Iris' started from uncertainty about a relationship, which she knew symbolized stability to her. The projection appeared in the middle of the session, so we didn't do the written part of the process, to avoid interrupting the regression.

In this example, note how the childhood episode transformed into something much earlier *as soon as Iris went into her own body in the past.* I suspect it was a conception moment, because of the feeling of walking towards the light (the sperm's approach to the egg feels that way) and the sense of male-female duality, which is common at this first contact. Couples' problems often are re-enactments of conception, with the partners seeing themselves as egg or sperm depending on the circumstances, and regardless of gender. For more about dealing with dualities, see the next section.

Iris: ...I see myself at six years old.

Paula: Do you see your six-year-old self 'out there', or are you inside her body?

Iris: She's out there.

Paula: Merge with her. Bring her to you and put her on like a sweater, until you see out of her eyes.

I: I've got it... I'm walking towards some light. There's a familiar uncertainty, but I'm moving forward anyway. This is my way, this is what I always do.

...Now I see him. My partner. He's so powerful. He's got all the power.

P: Look at him closely; think how he looks to you.

I: Yes: very powerful. Full of blue light. I can't have any power because he has so much. He has all of it.

P: Now make an imaginary voodoo doll or something three-dimensional and neutral, and transfer to it all that blue light and all that power that you can't have.

I: Okay, I'm done.

P: Now merge with that figure you've just made. Don't merge with your lover, just with the doll that has all his qualities pasted on it.

I: I've got that. [Breathes harder.]

P: Any new sensations, or intensified ones?

I: There's a lot of sexual energy... A duality, masculine-feminine.

P: Stay right in the middle of that duality, neither choosing the masculine nor the feminine, just be on the cusp of choosing.

I: [Growing bewilderment] Oh... They're both ME!!!

...I didn't know I could *go home* and *be powerful* at the same time! I thought I had to choose one or the other!

P: What is it like now?

I: There's electric energy, light blue and quiet. A sense of home, white, pure. The power is cobalt blue, not bad but very intense.

P: Where is that sense of intensity?

I: In my solar plexus.

P: Just stay with that for a moment; love yourself as the intensity of that cobalt-blue power.

I: [Tears] Mom is so weak and scared; I had to be small for her...

P: How's the power now?

I: A lot more solid, quiet. Feels like home.

The next example is from a student, working on herself shortly after I'd developed this technique.

I kept having trouble with a woman in my theatre group. I'm not sure why, but time after time, I'd make some comment on how we should interpret a certain passage or how we could improve technique, and I always ended up offending her; it was always contrary to how she saw that particular problem. No matter how careful I was, it would happen once or twice at each rehearsal. We'd been working together for some years with no major friction, then this pattern started quite suddenly. I tried reasoning that she's in the middle of a difficult spiritual quest herself and maybe she's unconsciously threatened by the fact that I'm doing all this transformational work... I tried my best communication skills... She'd get offended anyway. Then I decided to try the projection exercise on it.

It felt weird to stop being compassionate and understanding. I asked myself, what do I really think? Then I let loose, and started writing furiously, underlining every other word: "Dammit, she *does* have tacky ideas! She always sees it all wrong! I'm tired of being so understanding, she's *too loud* and *too red* and her mouth is *too big* and anyway my ideas are *right* and she's *wrong*!"

It felt scary, and deliciously wicked, and yet I knew what was coming next. I knew whom I really was describing. So, I pasted all that loudness and tackiness and mouthiness on a grey blob and merged with that. Became that, loved myself as that. I became big and flamboyant... and scared.

I think it was the moment when the egg gets formed, when all the parts of that cell come together. I'm Heart, coming into something that has never seen emotions, joining the Mind-brain I think, who feels very dignified and correct and cultured. I'm just too goddamn vivid, to paraphrase Tom Robbins. I'm ashamed. There's no room here for what I am.

I stay with that for what seems like an impossibly long time. Keep cycling through different aspects of it. It seems it will never end. Then a rapid transformation: a lot of light and a feeling of peace and if I look at N... she's just herself, she doesn't feel annoying anymore.

I felt a little trepidation going to the next rehearsal. I kept quiet most of the evening, but at one point I couldn't help making one comment and N... sided with me! I don't think we've had that kind of disagreement ever since.

Dilemmas

Sometimes, in the middle of a healing, we find ourselves faced with an impossible choice. We're damned if we do and we're damned if we don't. The classic dilemma is the placenta's, at birth: "If this baby is born, I die. If this baby is not born, he will die, and since I'm a part of him, I will die also."

In such circumstances, it's tempting to choose what we think is the right answer, from our adult viewpoint: of course the baby must be born. I must reconcile myself with the loss.

Seems obvious? Think again. When one chooses this course, one must still contend with that loss, *and* with the belief that the loss *must* happen in the first place.

In my own explorations, I found by chance that if, instead, I stayed in the exact moment of the dilemma, the moment just before that choice is made, the very cusp of the decision, after a (very uncomfortable) while, either the correct choice would become blindingly obvious, or else an incredible reframing would suddenly occur. The answer usually turned out to be neither A nor B. Either it resolved into some third, glorious solution, or the question itself would turn out to be moot.

My favourite example is still that of the very first time I met an impossible choice.

> I started with a back injury from lifting a deceased patient, a man I had known for many years and whom I'll call Jim. (I'm a volunteer firefighter and paramedic, so sometimes, unfortunately, I'm called upon to do this.) The pain in my lower back wasn't healing on its own, so one day I focused on it; I had tried sinking into the pain, before, with no success, so this time I went to the moment *just before* the injury: the moment of awkwardly reaching and lifting in a cramped space. I found myself standing at the top of what seemed like a bottomless chasm. I felt intense guilt, and to my horror I realized that I'd probably just lifted, in the same awkward way, what felt like a dying twin: another egg that presumably didn't make it past implantation. Most likely I was at the entrance of the womb. Had I pushed the other egg to its death? And I had to jump too, didn't I? So here was the dilemma: "If I jump down this huge cliff, I will surely die; but if I don't jump, I won't implant and I'll surely die."
>
> As an adult, of course, I knew that I had to jump. There was no way I could continue gestation unless I went over the edge and into the womb. But even from a grownup's perspective, I couldn't bring myself to imagine doing it. So I stayed on the edge, clinging and trembling with fear and guilt. Right on the point of decision, not deciding one way or the other. It lasted a while... It usually does. What happened next absolutely floored me. Somehow I asked, "What would I do if I didn't have this trauma?" And then a flash and a radical change of scene: "I would dive after you, Jim!" For the womb had suddenly transformed from a dark bottomless pit to a full, life-giving ocean! I dived with delight into warm, welcoming blue waves.
>
> Shortly after this, by the way, I found out that my fear of heights had vanished!

This was such an amazing experience that I took to treating every dilemma the same way. It's fascinating: you never know what the solution will turn out to be; the only constant is the feeling of euphoria when you finally make the right choice. In the example of Iris's session, in the previous section, we approached the feeling of masculine/feminine duality the same way. Oh, the wonder on Iris's face when that duality resolved. ("They're both *me*!)

Recently, I tried the same technique for a present-day dilemma. As I expected, it promptly led me into a prenatal trauma with the same flavour. The resolution wasn't electrifying, but I did get my problem resolved in a way that surprised me and that I still feel comfortable with.

I didn't stay in the middle for the whole session: there came a time where I couldn't stand it, so I moved to the side that felt 'right', the side of duty. It was interesting to see how, once the worst of the loss healed, I spontaneously returned to the middle. That was unexpected. There's also an example of a projection caught on the fly in the middle of the session.

The timing of the final phone call is a sort of miracle I've come to expect in this work. Note also how the other person's stance changed while, unknown to her, I worked on myself. Here are excerpts of my session notes:

> Louise just called, surprising me with the offer of sharing an art show with her, the summer after next. I'm extraordinarily honoured, as I admire her work so much, but haven't had time to paint recently; all my spare time has gone to the Institute. I was even thinking of withdrawing my membership to the gallery... I have only a few hours to decide yes or no. The booking has to happen today.
>
> Later: I've been feeling the problem from the middle, from the cusp of the dilemma. What I got so far is that I'm losing something dear to me, no matter what I do. If I say yes, I rob some time from healing work and from whatever I'm 'supposed to do.' If I say no, I'm leaving aside something I love to do in this world. Tightness in my heart, solar plexus, back.
>
> ...I'm at a place where to step forward is to lose something, forever. Visual: a gap between two vertical, slightly convex, surfaces. [Maybe first cell division?]
>
> Duty to world / duty to self. I stay in the middle.
>
> Now I'm two vertical cliffs, side by side. Phrase: "It's wrong, no matter what."
>
> I'm split apart and trying to run away from the question, trying to solve it by not caring. I'm two cliffs, separating and trying to reach back to each other.
>
> I see J's daughter. Just met her last night and was instantly charmed. I understand she's a projection here. What do I see in her? Innocence, strength, beauty, commitment, resourcefulness. I merge into those qualities. They're me, of course. Mind and Crown brain? Lots of grief.
>
> ...Louise is due to call. I'm running out of time. I move to the side of 'no', to the side of duty, because I'm not getting anywhere by sitting in the middle. I pretend I've decided to say no. I add the sense of time pressure to the mix.
>
> Instantly, an explosion of grief. I have failed.
>
> I have failed myself, I've failed my innocent side, the creative side of me I had projected on J's daughter. Ribs feel numb; part of me seems to be dying. Phrase: "It's time to die."
>
> Grief releases. Change of scene. I'm back in the middle, not deciding. "It's the only way to attend to myself."

Brighter. More playful. More 'yes'. Nature, birds, playful life. Somehow time constraints resolve?

Eleven o'clock. Still numb in ribs. Some part of me is so damaged that I can hardly access it, but I still feel a cautious yes. I don't know how I'll find the time to do both healing and painting, but the whole world seems to tell me, lightly, playfully, that it'll sort itself out.

11:01: Louise calls. Apologizing profusely for being late. I laugh and tell her she's exactly on time. I tell her my cautious yes and she tells me her own change of heart: that she's okay with some uncertainty on my part and willing to do the show solo if I can't participate.

This method has turned out to be a very safe way to proceed. But I must warn you here about an experiment Grant did with some students, and which turned out to be unsafe. They used two opposite sensations (in their case, the sensations of being in a peak experience in a moment the past, versus those of their average state of consciousness in the present) and played with jumping rapidly and repeatedly from one extreme to the other — from one time to another. After a few minutes, several of them realized that they were feeling somewhat blank or spaced out. One student, who had been in a peak state, felt his peak state dissolve into blankness! They had to work hard to heal that blankness, just to return to normal; that was a drag. The problem seems to be more about *time jumping* than jumping between two possible scenarios, but there also have been cautions from therapists who used that method of jumping repeatedly between pairs of polarities and ended up with excessively spaced-out clients. To stay on the safe side, here's the caution:

When healing dilemmas or polarized situations, do not flip repeatedly between the two opposite sides of the problem - especially if the two sides are separated in time. Rather, stay in the middle, in the cusp between the two extremes. If this seems too difficult, then just choose one side and stay there.

In my first example above, 'jumping between the opposites' would have meant going to the situation where I jumped down the cliff, then after a short while going back to a scenario where I chose to die atop the cliff, then return to jumping, then return to staying, and so on, like flipping back and forth between two movies on a TV. It's *much safer* to stay in the cusp of the decision. If for some reason you cannot stand that, (or the healing stalls, as happened in my second example) then choose only one side and heal from that viewpoint.

Structures in your Body

Rarely, you might see or sense solid objects in your body during a regression. These might feel like rods or rubber bands connecting points together, or containers enclosing an area, or geometric shapes made of extruded plastic.

We know very little about this phenomenon. There have been instances where these structures were associated with physical pain and some chronic illnesses. Grant mentions the case history of a client who had severe acne, which they traced to a structure pulling at her liver.[31]

The structures can be healed the usual way, by focusing on the discomfort associated with them and regressing, and healing the associated traumas. The objects dissolve when the trauma releases. But there's a curious, faster way that sometimes gives results: if you love yourself as the area just above your forehead, the object usually dissolves rapidly.

Why does this work? The area just above your forehead is the seat of what we call the Buddha brain or crown brain. We don't know much about this brain's specific function, but it seems related to our spiritual outlook, to our interface with 'outside'. What can this possibly have to do with constructing these weird objects? We don't yet know. Be it as it may, this brain seems to really want to help, and it does so by building energetic structures; the problem is that the structures sometimes stay in place long after they have served their purpose. By focusing your attention into your crown brain, and loving yourself as it, you help it release the misunderstanding that caused it to do this in the first place.

Tal mentioned a client who had begun having back pains while she was pregnant. The pain didn't stop after the birth - a year later it was still present. "We found a Buddha structure at the injury site. It seems that her Buddha brain thought she needed some support, as her back was under pressure; and it just stayed on."

I only encountered this phenomenon twice in my explorations. The first time, it felt like metallic rods, tipped with tiny balls, had appeared in my chest. They looked like strange implants, the sort of thing you'd see in a sci-fi movie. This was, as I recall, in the middle of a birth trauma. The second example was at the time when all the brains come together to form the egg. There's a moment when the energy meridians are formed. I

---

[31] *The Basic Whole-Hearted Healing Manual*, p.68.

found myself enclosed in a network of metallic tubes, crudely patched together. Seemed like my little crown brain was trying to help me construct this network of meridians with the spiritual equivalent of recycled steel pipes and duct tape.

In both instances, bringing my centre of awareness into my crown brain and loving myself for the misguided behaviour was enough to dissolve the structures in a minute or two. (Note that I was already regressed to the originating trauma in the past. This trick doesn't work as well if you do it from the point of view of a physical discomfort in the present, because the originating trauma is still active.)

A new student, in his first session, found that much of his torso seemed enclosed in a sort of bottle. I immediately thought of applying this Crown brain trick, but his healing was progressing rapidly, even though he simply focused on the bottle itself and on its contents. It dissolved without special intervention. This man used to carry a lot of tension in his torso. This has noticeably lessened now, although one can't necessarily credit it to this session. A great deal of self-care and lifestyle changes attended the improvement.

Transpersonal Experiences and Peak States

These are what makes it all worthwhile!

Sometimes, as a trauma clears, you suddenly find yourself experiencing something more drastic than the usual (and already pleasant) sense of being calm, peaceful, lightweight, large and bright. There are many, many examples of these experiences, ranging from feelings of peace or happiness to unity with the natural world or a sense of divinity. The most important thing to remember is that all these experiences are our birthright. They are normal. The average state of consciousness that is prevalent in our culture is what's abnormal.

We call these wonderful occurrences peak experiences (if they're transient) and peak states (if they're permanent). Yes, most of them can, and should, be permanent.

Now, here's why the concept of the triune brains is such a big deal: when the brains finally resolve their differences and work in harmony, they fuse together and become as one. The characteristics of the resulting peak states are the same for everyone. I will dwell briefly on these particular peak states here, because they're the ones you're most likely to encounter at this level of healing.

When the mind brain fuses with the heart brain, we get a peak state called Inner Peace. Past traumas do not get triggered in people who are in this state, at least not in an emotional way. (People in Inner Peace can still access and heal traumas by starting from physical sensations.) If there's also an intact connection to the Creator, Inner Peace becomes the Beauty Way. There's a sense of loveliness and wonder to everything; even rags and garbage display a sort of beauty.

When the heart and body brains fuse together, we get a state we call Underlying Happiness. While the normal range of emotions remains, they occur over a background of happiness and love.

When the crown brain, mind, heart, solar plexus and body all fuse together, we get the Hollow state. One's body feels like air and there's a sense of comfort and ease to everything, added to the sensations of Inner Peace and Underlying Happiness.

When the spine brain and placenta also fuse, one gets a state of Wholeness.

Lesser versions of these states occur when the fusion between the brains is partial. And a host of other peak states occur when we restore our harmony with other aspects of the world. See Grant's book *Peak States of Consciousness: Theory and Applications*, Volume 1 for a lot more information. The main point to remember here is that all these experiences are normal; they are the way we're supposed to be. Traumas block them, so when we heal the right trauma we stumble into them again.

All peak experiences and peak states should be comfortable even if they're extremely intense. Any discomfort is caused by... yes, you guessed it: trauma. Ask yourself where the discomfort is located, figure out the emotional tone, and heal it like any other trauma, no matter how intense it is.

If the experience seems transpersonal, but overwhelmingly intimidating, check for the presence of an archetypal image and heal it immediately. Our body brains, in particular, are very adept at pretending they are God. They can generate very convincing images of mightily dangerous spirits. Don't worry: merge with it, own it, heal it. It's just you: an aspect of you, in disguise. If there's a genuine impression of divinity here, it is absolutely safe to merge with it, too, so you can't go wrong with this one.

Often the experience is transient. In general, healing the remaining traumas in the same moment in the past will stabilize it into a peak state. Some experiences remain transient by nature: we call them gateway

events. To return to this experience, you need to regress again to the moment where the experience first appeared.
Here's an example of approaching and attaining a gateway event, from my own healing notes. Notice how the ship first appears as a metaphor of trauma, then shows up again as a metaphor of harmony.

> Started the session from feelings of being a misfit in a group of people at a dinner party. Tightness in solar plexus. The feeling is "Nobody here knows who I am." At that party, I had spent the evening wanting to hide under the table.
>
> I stay in solar plexus's sensations. Loud music in my head. Solar plexus makes a curtain out of this music. Mère doesn't know she's pregnant with me. I'm still incognito... just like last night at table.
>
> More light. Big wave of fear.
>
> The light is sacred.
>
> "You are sacred." My solar plexus hears this.
>
> I'm on the floor, pregnant, sick.
>
> Now I'm an earth goddess, destitute.
>
> I'm Mère, implanting me, not wanting to, and yet knowing I'm precious.
>
> [I move to the floor, to better track the sensations by adopting the position my past self is in.]
>
> I'm on the deck of a ship that's sinking in a storm.
>
> Now Mère has conceived and knows she holds me... We'll somehow be whole, she and I. But solar plexus is still holding back from implanting. "I can't do this without your wish."
>
> Mère as earth goddess.
>
> I can't do this halfway. It's my whole body or nothing. I can't decide to implant 'just a little bit.' Love myself for my reluctance.
>
> Finally I expand. Solar plexus is lit up and open like a bag for the first time in ages... or ever? I'm a huge ship, rocking crazily, but the sails are good and everything's tidy. I'm gigantic. It's like... an ark? Like a picture of Noah's ark, seen in cut-out view... except it's the whole planet! I'm the whole thing, and I'm a passenger, all at once. I've read of other people seeing the earth consciousness as a big apartment building with a compartment for each species... but it's not a condo, it's a ship! And it's the whole planet, sailing through space...

I saw different views of this beautiful Earth-Ark whenever traumas resolved in my next few sessions, all about implantation. I can recall the experience in a vivid way whenever I wish by recreating this atmosphere inside me: essentially by regressing to that implantation moment. That specific implantation moment, then, is a gateway to experiencing the biosphere as this gigantic Ark (others have reported another gateway to that experience at birth). This isn't a peak state per se, but the experience does colour my perception of the world in a permanent way.

Whenever you have any of these experiences, it's important to make a note of the last trauma moment you healed. If the experience or peak state becomes inaccessible again, you may be able to regain it by going back to that moment and healing any remaining traumas.[32]

Often, leftover traumas show up as resistance to the wonderful experience itself! Here is a short example from a workshop student I'll call Miriam. We were healing a portion of the formation of the egg. This is a moment when the heart, mind and crown brains descend into the body and solar plexus. Several students were already in a state of expansion and light.

> "I'm moving into the state... but now I worry that if I'm in this expanded state, I'll be too emotional, too 'out there', too much to handle."
> "That sounds like a reasonable fear from your body's point of view, doesn't it? After all, it sees Heart, the seat of emotions, for the first time."
> "You mean this is still about the past?"
> "Of course. Where is that fear situated?"
> "In my heart area."
> "Okay, love yourself from your heart, for the fear of being 'too much'."
> "... Yes, the fear's gone now, and I feel even lighter!"

As you see, it's very easy to attribute the resistance to our present situation. It's useful to remember that whenever we are not calm, peaceful and light, we are actually stuck somewhere in the past. While I moved into my first peak states, I had whole list of objections to heal before I could enjoy each of them fully: "I don't deserve this." "All this light is for spiritual people, for gurus or priests, not for someone like me." "I feel so bright, I'm lit up like a Christmas tree! What will people think?" All these objections turned out to be from leftover traumas related to the 'big one' that had blocked the peak state.

---

[32] Sometimes, this is not enough, because the traumas blocking the state are too numerous, or so severe that we don't feel safe bringing them to consciousness. This is where a peak state therapist can help. There is a list of them on our website.

No Time to Finish

If you run out of time, it's useful to remember that the healing you've done so far will not reverse itself. Your work isn't lost. Even black holes will stay put, partly healed, and ancestors will politely wait for your return - if you can find that exact moment again. The challenge comes when we have to return to the present, to the busyness of daily life, with some big past trauma fully activated. Here are a few tricks to ease the misery:

1) Quit on the win. Each big trauma is composed of several related aspects. Learn to identify the moments of respite where one aspect of the problem has let go, and the next aspect is coming in. There's often a short interval of light and relief. Take advantage of one of these to return to the present.

2) Use gratitude and loving yourself. Gratitude puts us squarely into the present. So, as you open your eyes and reorient yourself to the room around you, find something to be grateful about. Even a very small thing will do. Then magnify the feeling of gratitude and let it flood your whole body. And as we saw earlier, it doesn't matter who you're grateful to: gratitude itself is what changes you. Add the Loving-Yourself technique to boost that gratitude's effects.

3) Reassure your past self (or the ancestor you're healing) that you will return. To make sure you'll be able to find the same trauma again, note down the problem you started from, the atmosphere of the time and place to which you regressed, the emotions and body sensations. Rereading your healing notes is the surest way to bring yourself back to an unfinished trauma. This is especially important with holes, because we invest so much energy in hiding them from our own consciousness.

Chapter 5

Increasing your Skill: Common Obstacles and How to Overcome Them

Chapters 3 and 4 already showed you some tips to help you access and release traumas, but there are some that are worth reiterating, and a few new ones I'd like to mention. This chapter is intended to help you trouble-shoot your sessions. What should you do if you know you have a problem but can't access the traumatic feelings? What can be done to speed the release of something that really feels stuck? And what about healing physical problems? These are huge topics, with many unknowns, but here are a few of the answers we do have, in synoptic form.

Several of these strategies use tools from other healing modalities. For a student wishing to advance further, or a therapist interested in using our work, I strongly recommend further reading about and training in those modalities.

Difficulties in Accessing the Trauma

Loving yourself

As always, the Loving-Yourself technique is the best tool to lower your resistance to feeling. It seems so pedestrian, yet it's so powerful. Use this technique to generate some unconditional love in yourself; love yourself exactly as you are, without any agenda to change. Love yourself for not wanting to feel. This technique seems to melt resistance away.

Exception: Underlying Happiness

A curious exception to the above can occur for people whose heart and body brains are functioning in harmony, a peak state we call Underlying Happiness (see the section on transpersonal experiences and peak states in last chapter). When I entered that state, I found that if I cranked up that feeling of loving myself, the background state of happiness would also magnify, and although I could still feel the physical tension, the negative emotions would remain buried. To this day, I can sit for hours with a leaden weight in my heart, flooding it with that bright happiness and loving, and nothing else happens. This is not the same as healing. Stalling is what it is! The way around it is to *wait until you feel the emotions before starting to focus on loving yourself*. Then, if the traumatic emotions seem fragile, make that self-love very low key. Imagine you're entering the room of a person who is gravely ill. You enter on tiptoes with a softly glowing candle of love, and leave the fanfare of happiness at the door.

Again, this is *only* valid for people who have the Underlying Happiness state. It's possible to have it (and any other peak state) right from birth, in which case you wouldn't necessarily know about it. If you're the sort of person who tends to be easily happy, *and* you have trouble accessing traumas because you feel so goddamn positive, try this technique. For all other people, the Loving Yourself technique does help accessing traumatic emotions.

Inner Peace

The Inner Peace peak state, where the mind and heart function in harmony, can also cause problems in accessing past traumas. In any given workshop group, we usually have one or two people who come in saying they have tried all sorts of healing modalities and can never access past emotions. Usually, upon testing, we find that they naturally have the Inner Peace state. In this state, emotions from past traumas do not get activated; the person tends to stay emotionally in the present.

Fortunately, there's an easy way around this: when past traumas get triggered, they show up as physical tension or discomfort. Simply think about the issue you'd like to heal, focus on it, write about it; then scan your body for tightness, pain, discomfort, pinching sensations, or sensations of movement. Next, magnify that physical sensation a bit (unless it's already overwhelming!) and sink into it. The emotional tone of it will soon become apparent. Note that in certain peak states, emotions are more like thoughts. Emotions do not need to be overwhelming for you to work on them. See also my example about working with a reduced emotional range on page 62.

Timing

The time of day often makes a difference to the ease in accessing traumas. In general, we tend to be less defended in the morning, more emotionally fragile, and this greatly eases healing. In the evening, the opposite is true. In my case, that Underlying Happiness is much stronger in the late evenings... That's when it's easiest to stall and completely forget to look for traumatic emotions. In general, the best time to heal is whenever you're feeling bad. And the worst time to heal is when you're feeling really, really fine... Who wants to hunt down fear and sadness when the going's good?

Suspending disbelief

From Tal: "Students often get caught up in not believing what they see in regression, especially pre-natal memories, or encountering lights and such phenomena. This impedes the healing, because they spend most of the time (out of body!) looking at it and trying to make sense of it, and end up with nothing. I tell them to remember how they perceive when they see a film. Even in the most far-fetched fantasy or sci-fi picture, you let yourself believe, for two hours, that it is all true. In the professional jargon, it is called suspension of disbelief. When in regression, use this mechanism that we all exercise in the theatre. Take good notes, and wait till later to analyse what is real and what is not. It seems to work with students who claim to have this problem."

Prejudice about what the trauma might be

Sometimes we have trouble accessing traumatic content because we have already made up our minds about what the trauma might be. I focus on prenatal and perinatal traumas in this manual because that's overwhelmingly where COEXes lead us, but some traumas do have their roots in the near past. Do not dismiss anything.

At other times, the problem stems from a misunderstanding of what constitutes an emotion. Blankness is an emotion, so is indecision, so is 'being irritated at myself because I can't find the trauma', so is 'being convinced that I'm doing this all wrong,' so is distractedness, so is sleepiness. Sleepiness and a wandering mind are an indication that something big is just around the corner. I find that a quick, stream-of-consciousness scanning of the contents of the distraction and mind-wandering will often show me aspects of the trauma, just in the same way a dream does.

See also the section on using the EFT psychological reversal step, below.

Distraction from a bigger trauma

Suppose you've decided to continue working on a certain issue, which we'll label Issue X. One morning you just can't get into Issue X even though you know there are still dregs of it left, and you really want to clean it up… Ok, stop and consider what's on your mind, then. More often than not, you'll find that there's another issue distracting you. Let's call it Issue Y. Issue Y seems irrelevant, it's not serious, it's not the same thing, forget it; I really, really want to clean up Issue X *first.*

Can't get anywhere? Then heal issue Y. Get it out of the way. Now, you want to make a bet? Then bet that inside this seemingly unrelated Issue Y you'll find an overlooked aspect of Issue X. Such is the way we create our world. I stumble into this phenomenon quite regularly, and it's wonderful.

Using the problems popping up in your daily life

More on the same theme. It really is remarkable how we draw to ourselves manifestations of the issue that occupies us. If you have a partially resolved trauma whose remaining aspects you can't access, just watch for the small upsets in your daily life. Then heal the disturbing emotions from those. More often than not, you'll find that they are indeed expressions of the remaining trauma. This is one of the aspects of long-term self-exploration that most fascinate me. We really do want to heal, to be whole. And we really can manifest just the right triggers in our lives.

Note that those triggers don't have to be big. You don't have to let them *become* big. My colleague John Heinegg quotes this from an unknown source: "First, Spirit whispers. Next, it shouts. Then, it hits you on the head with a baseball bat." We don't have to wait for the baseball bat (the car accident, the divorce, the pneumonia) to heal. Hints of discomfort will lead us right back to the core issue we're working on.

Considering the worst-case scenario

Sometimes we really *do* know what the trauma is. We have an image in the back of our minds, pushed in a corner, with a tiny label attached: "Please, let it not be so."

Ask yourself what's the worst thing that could happen, or that could have happened in the past. Is there anything you particularly don't want the trauma to be about?

A friend who was physically very ill told me at the beginning of our session that she really, really hoped that this regression wouldn't give her feelings of nausea and wouldn't make her throw up. Oh well... Minutes later she had to reach for a bucket.

Another client, who was hoping to heal on his own, approached a birth trauma. All his current problems seemed to converge into one particular moment, which he kept circling around but couldn't get into. At one point, he mentioned that the one thing he most feared and most wanted to avoid was a scenario where the umbilical cord was wrapped around his neck. The remark popped out unprovoked; why? Probably because that was indeed the trauma waiting to be unveiled in the past. This client eventually had to stop using Whole-Hearted Healing because, as he circled around and around the core trauma without daring to face it directly, he was getting more and more suicidal. The hazard was compounded because he had a very limited array of coping skills, and was unwilling, due to very negative experiences with mental health professionals, to organize proper support for himself.[33]

I saw an example of this blocking of the worst-case scenario in my own work recently. This also was near birth, as the placenta releases its hold on life and transfers its 'essence' into the baby. I wasn't able to access the next piece of the puzzle; the healing had stalled for days. Meanwhile I'd been mulling over dark fears about environmental catastrophes... The image was of being exiled and having to leave my home, walking down a path in the wilderness with other exiles... One morning I bit the bullet and overlaid this stuck image on my equally stuck placental death trauma... Oh yes. The 'exiled ' feeling was the placenta's own! The 'path' was the cord, leading me into my 'baby body'... After an extremely intense release of emotions, the picture changed

---

[33] Wrapped-cord traumas are one of the main causes of suicidal feelings arising during regression, though we now have evidence that another, very early trauma sets us up for this. So far, we've mostly seen the suicidal feelings arise in people who had already felt suicidal in the past, before they tried WHH, though one man became suicidal with no warning and no previous history. (The main thing that kept him alive was puzzlement: he couldn't figure out why he so much wanted to die while he had a good job, loads of friends and a wonderful place to live.)

It is entirely possible to heal this, but be warned that the self-destructive feelings can be intense and violent, and can arise either during a session or between sessions (triggered, for instance, by feelings of rejection in the present.)

To heal the traumas without danger to yourself, you need an excellent support network (our workshop trainees use a buddy system), and what I'll call, for lack of better words, a mature or seasoned attitude towards your suicidal feelings. This means that you're able to maintain a certain sense of detachment and curiosity, even when the going gets tough, and that you have a good, diversified array of coping skills. I'm afraid that this has nothing to do with willpower; it has everything to do with the severity of the past traumas. So please be honest with yourself in your self-assessment. Your life could literally be in the balance. *To approach the traumas susceptible to trigger suicidal feeling under these conditions, you still need caution and support. You must also agree to take complete responsibility for whatever happens to you, as outlined in the liability agreement at the beginning of this book.*

If many intense traumas to date seem to overwhelm you in the present, or if, during suicidal episodes in the past, you needed outside intervention so you wouldn't actually harm yourself, then *extreme caution and 24-hour supervision* are needed to approach this type of trauma in regression. The supervision *must* be maintained for a few days after you think you've healed the trauma, because sometimes other aspects cycle back during this period. If this is not possible, then *immediately stop using Whole-Hearted Healing or any other regression therapy.* Other peak state processes, such as the 15-minute Miracle, are much safer for you.

drastically. I now have a greater sense of wholeness, and although I'm still not entirely reassured about the fate of the planet, that particular dark fear is gone.

Dreams

The emotional fallout from dreams can also help trigger you into deeper healing. Disregard the plot, consider that all the characters in the dream are aspects of you, and use the emotional content of each character to propel yourself into feeling more intensely. One could do an entire healing practice just based on working with dreams.

Music

Healing to music invariably propels us deeper inwards, but there is a catch: no music is really innocuous. There is no such thing as neutral, generic music that will just help you relax and tune in to your emotions: music will do that, but depending on its atmosphere and the distribution of the tones, and also on its connotations in your own life, it will stimulate this or that area of your body, this or that type of emotion, or this or that developmental event. Creation stories often speak of gods singing the world into being... And sure enough, some melodies will make people spontaneously regress - everyone to the same developmental event! It seems that part of the biological instructions that we get as we grow can be translated as music... And some especially sensitive people can hear it - including some well-known composers. In fact, one could argue that a good number of the melodies that perennially catch people's imagination are derived from developmental event music. Other traditions use music to stimulate different parts of the body; there are several collections of chakra-tuning music. So choosing music at random is most likely to distract you from the trauma you're trying to heal, or even to trigger another traumatic theme that you're not necessarily prepared to handle just now.

It's another matter if you have music cycling around and around in your head. If it's a song, pay attention to the words and their emotional content; they may simply be yet another metaphor thrown at you by your mind brain: another form of self-talk. Scan it for content, and let it go. If it won't let go, try singing it. Sing one phrase at a time, healing whatever it triggers. Do the same for simple melodies without words.

If it's written in fugue style, though, you're in trouble. Some stuff is just too complex to hum. Then go ahead and play a recording of that music. Check whether it is relevant to the trauma you're trying to access: sometimes we play music in our head to *avoid* the issue! If it does seem relevant, it is, most likely, a piece whose emotional content matches that of the stuck trauma. Or else it matches the atmosphere of the developmental event you're stuck at. Either way, keep listening and healing until every note can wash right through you without causing distress.

Using breath

With deepest apologies to the highly trained practitioners of diverse rebirthing and breathwork therapies, I will oversimplify here and suggest that certain patterns of breathing help trigger past emotions. Slight hyperventilating, in particular, seems to break down our defences. It also seems to assist in releasing toxins (such as the anaesthetics used during your birth) out of your system. There may be great potential in combining the principles of breathwork with Whole-Hearted Healing's concepts of staying in-body and continuing to heal long enough. The next chapter will return to these possibilities.

Holding breath

Grant devised this method, and the late Dr. Adam Waisel refined it. When approaching birth traumas, if you are unable to face the experience completely, holding your breath can stimulate the intense panic of that moment. I *do not* recommend Grant's technique unless you're *sure* that you have no cardiac or respiratory problems. It simply involves emptying your lungs of air, and holding your breath while pinching your nose shut, until you can't stand it. The panic will show up in a precise physical location. As soon as you have located it, resume breathing normally. You may have to redo the exercise again after healing the first trauma. Typically that panic will appear in several different locations in sequence. Each location corresponds to a trauma.

Adam came up with a more gentle and less hazardous version of this no-breath technique: he discovered that for most people, merely holding the nose shut while breathing shallowly through the mouth was enough to trigger the birth panic. In both cases, use the technique only once you've already regressed to birth and can't quite get into the traumas.

Viewing

'Viewing' is one aspect of Traumatic Incident Reduction (TIR), developed by Dr. Frank Gerbode and the Institute for Metapsychology. I'll let Grant briefly describe the technique's intended use:

> "Essentially, what you do is run over the entire trauma moment by moment, in as much detail as you can. You consciously start before the trauma began, run through the incident, then repeat it again and again as many times as necessary. Generally one finds that nothing hurts at first, then more of the memory comes to light, then the pain increases, reaches a crescendo, and quickly ends. Staying in your chest and body speeds the process. I've found this technique invaluable with certain traumas I just couldn't feel."[34]

Although I've never applied TIR in its integral form, I sometimes hijack the Viewing idea to clean up traumas that I can clearly recall as finite events. For example, I used it to heal a moment in my young adulthood when someone attacked me. It was easy to recall the event and heal the main aspects of it directly, but, since I really wanted to stop that pattern for good, I used a modification of the Viewing technique to run through the entire episode from beginning to end a few times. Whenever I found any instant of the event that still upset me, I would stop at that moment, freeze-frame it, and heal the emotional content before going on. It took several viewings to find all the aspects. Some were hidden in comparatively innocuous moments of the incident. All of them led to earlier events.

I'd like to highlight the difference between this and a very common avoidance tactic used, on occasion, even by seasoned students. I call this tactic 'going for a walk.' It consists in avoiding a trauma by ranging mentally in time or space around the injury. Just the other day, I talked a student out of exploring an ancestor's later life, reminding him to stay inside the one traumatic moment he'd found. Earlier, I witnessed a venerable member of our Institute, going exploring around and up the axis of a strange disc we'd discovered, then wondering why his traumas

---

[34] *The Whole-Hearted Healing Manual,* p. 25.

about the disc didn't release.[35] Another way to 'go for a walk' is ranging from brain to brain instead of staying in the most injured one. Use Viewing to access traumas, but when you've found one, stay put until you've healed it; only then should you walk a little further. Or else go walking all the way: use the Viewing technique in its intended application, as Grant described it above.[36]

Strategies from Body-Centred therapies

Aside from clearly describing problems and solutions about loving ourselves, Gay and Kathlyn Hendricks have done great work with body-centered therapy. In their book *At the Speed of Life*, they describe a host of strategies for accessing traumas. One of them involves becoming aware of, and magnifying, the small nervous movements we make when we are triggered but cannot access the trauma. A therapist notes, for example, nervous toe tapping in a client who is describing a current problem. Then he says something like, "That tapping you do with your foot? No, no, don't stop; in fact, do just a little more of that." This brings one of the trauma's manifestations to consciousness. Magnifying the tapping, just slightly, allows the client to start accessing the emotion that the tapping attempts to mask.

Of course, all this is easier to observe from the outside, but it is still possible to speed up access to a blocked trauma by noticing our own body mannerisms. Then, instead of trying to quit the mannerism, we keep making it... but with full awareness of its role as one of the trauma's expressions. Inside the movement, or the tightness, or the holding, or the hunched back or the neck held at an angle, will be an emotional component of the originating trauma.

---

[35] Tal adds, "While you are still traumatized, your perceptions of the trauma moment are distorted, and so there is no way to really know where you are until it is healed. For all those who like exploring: play after work. First heal the trauma, and then take a look around. You get a more accurate picture anyway."

[36] In which case I'd recommend more training. See Gerald French and Chrys J. Harris, *Traumatic Incident Reduction*, CRC Press 1999. I particularly value this manual for its insights about communication between therapist and client. The principles are clearly explained and are useful for any power therapy.

In the same vein, Institute members have spoken glowingly about using strategies from Peter Levine's Somatic Experiencing to access and release traumas.[37]

Using the Psychological Reversal Step

We borrowed this one from Gary Craig's Emotional Freedom Technique or EFT. The Psychological Reversal step helps us to temporarily set aside our counter-commitments to healing.[38] You use a phrase, repeated three times, to trigger your body's objections to healing a trauma, and at the same time rub a small area directly below the centre of either clavicle (collarbone) - Gary Craig calls these areas the 'sore spots.' This action seems to temporarily cancel the effects of those counter-commitments. The phrase is "Even though I have this (*fill in the name of the problem*), I completely love and accept myself."

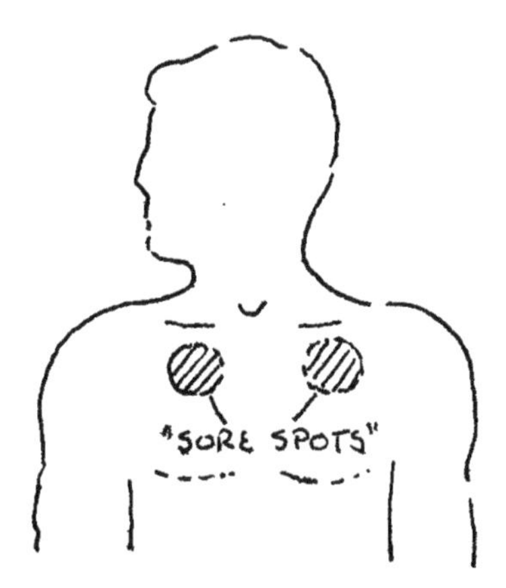

Figure 4: The 'sore spots' used for the psychological reversal step in EFT. (Adapted from www.emofree.com.)

---

[37] See *The Basic Whole-Hearted Healing Manual* p. 130-131, and Peter Levine's book, *Awakening the Tiger - Healing Trauma.*

[38] Grant notes: "It is actually 'turning off' traumas that cause you to think that you need this trauma that you are trying to heal." I think this is synonymous to what I wrote, but perhaps another wording will help.

I use this technique whenever there's resistance to accessing the trauma. I use it on distraction, sleepiness, the need to 'go for a walk', inability to stay inside my body. It opens a small window of opportunity - Tal says about 10 seconds if the resistance is great. Just enough time to really get into the trauma. Tal adds, "I had a few sessions in which I had to rub the spot continuously for the whole duration."

Here's an example of a session where we used the technique. The upsetting feelings 'all over my skin' are common right after birth, when a baby's skin first becomes exposed to air, and are seriously aggravated when the birth attendants attempt to scrape the vernix (the waxy layer protecting the baby) from her skin.

> Diana had asked me for some individual help because she always felt inadequate in workshop settings. We talked about how she felt and she decided that the dominant feeling was one of hopelessness. It rated as an 8 out of 10.
>
> "Put yourself in the situation of trying to heal something during the workshop."
>
> "There's a nervousness in my stomach... I imagine myself screaming in frustration. I see myself as a little baby. An angry feeling on my skin all over."
>
> "Are you inside yourself as this little baby or is she out there somewhere?"
>
> "I'm her. I'm inside... Now the anger's changed to fear and desperation."
>
> "Just love yourself as you are, with all this fear and desperation all over your skin."
>
> "...Now my skin is feeling some of the love.
>
> "Now there's a black ball of fear inside, and it says, Don't trust it, it'll never stay, it's probably wrong." [These were her themes when she got frustrated with healing.]
>
> "Okay. Merge with that black ball."
>
> "I can't. It feels like I don't know where I'll end up if I go into that black ball."
>
> "Okay. Try the psychological reversal step from EFT. Just that step."
>
> [Rubbing below clavicle] "Even though I don't know where I'll end up if I go into that black ball, I completely love and accept myself. Even though..." [Repeated 3 times.]
>
> "Try merging into that black ball now."
>
> "I'm there, I'm it. Inside, it says, I don't know I don't know I don't know...
>
> "...Now it feels like that 'I Don't Know' black ball is deflating, it's all worn out...
>
> "I just noticed how tight my body is."
>
> "Keep noticing that tightness while staying in that black ball."

"It's flattening... It's in my upper chest area. Now it's just a blob... I feel pressure into me, that flatness wants to go around something that's coming in." [Probably an earlier event, the time when the brains come together to form the egg or sperm.] "Anger again. I want to be wild and crazy, I want to break out of something... Now I'm hopeless, very dark. It's hard to stay with it."

"Try using that psychological reversal step again"

"Even though I can't stand staying in that dark, I completely love and accept myself... [3 times]

"... I want to run away! Exactly like during the workshop!"

"Okay. Love yourself for wanting to run away."

The 'wanting to run away' in her chest vanished, quickly replaced by the next trauma in line: more hopelessness, in her solar plexus this time.

"The hopelessness is my home, my cave. I'm sad, I just want to curl up and sleep; it's no good... I'm really sleepy, I can't focus anymore."

"Okay, try psychological reversal on the sleepiness."

"Even though I'm too sleepy to focus, I do completely love and accept myself. Even though..."

"Any change?"

"Yes, it's a lot easier now. There's a pile of very physical feelings... Distressed in legs and body, nausea... A huge shift into physical from emotional. Something's coming into me, from above. It's taking up a lot of space. [I'm guessing body brain joining with Solar Plexus, because of that shift to more physical sensations.] ...It's feeling less and less threatening now. Something has come in, it's completely encapsulated. The distress in my body has gone away."

There was more to the session, but this fragment shows the timing of using the psychological reversal step. It drastically speeds the access of trauma aspects we cannot stand to look at. One can also heal those feelings of resistance individually, but if the shortcut works, one might as well use it.

Scanning your body

I described in chapter 4 the technique of pressing briefly and gently into the area of physical discomfort to get an image of the trauma. The example was in the context of approaching a feeling of blankness or emptiness, but you can use that little technique on all sorts of things. Again, the image may seem impossibly brief and vague, but can be surprisingly useful in accessing the trauma.

If the sensations are so vague that you can't locate where the trauma is in your body, try running your hands slowly and lightly all over your skin. I find that when I do this, the traumatic emotions increase when my hand reaches the seat of the trauma.

All forms of bodywork are wonderful ways to access traumas. We will return to this in Chapter 6.

Using Image Streaming to get an image

Sometimes people get frustrated with not seeing anything, and at that point tend to give up. Here you can use elements of a technique called Image Streaming. Dr Win Wenger, of Project Renaissance, developed this technique to sharpen Inner Vision and improve creativity over time; but you can use the basic form with instant results. [39]

Let's say you see nothing. A common complaint... Fine: describe aloud the "nothing" that you see. Is it dark, bright, or in between? Dark? Okay. What kind of dark? Matte, opaque, transparent, solid and substantial, heavy, vast, confined? Keep defining it to yourself; more and more details soon become apparent; it's as if, by hearing yourself describe, your automatically know if the description is accurate and you self-correct and discriminate. Soon abstract shapes become apparent, and then there is enough visual information to find where in the abstracts "you" are, and continue with the healing. Keep an open mind: we often perceive metaphors first, and as the healing progresses and our comfort zone widens, the information feels more biological.

Difficulties in Releasing the Trauma

What if you have accessed the trauma successfully, but now you're just sitting in it and sitting in it and it isn't going away? First, make sure you have all the pieces: scan through the list of special situations in Chapter 1. Pay special attention to your surroundings. Are you copying emotions from someone else? Is there a hole hiding below the surface of your skin? Can you sense ancestors or other presences around you? If you really do have all the pieces of the puzzle, then try some of these tricks to speed the release of the trauma.

---

[39] Dr. Wenger's website, www.winwenger.com, offers extensive material on this process and its many applications.

Making sure you are in your body

This is as basic as it gets, yet it is by far the most common obstacle to the release of traumas. We forget to stay in our body in the past. Tal notes, "Sometimes people are just partially in-body. Even of you are 80% in-body, the healing will take forever. It is easy to miss." Make sure your awareness includes the whole area of the injury.

Interestingly, this problem is more common in people who have good visual perceptions. The tendency is to place the injury site in front of you, in order to watch how it's doing. Give up on seeing for the time being: make sure the image is completely you, and you are completely the image.

Loving yourself

How can I say it enough? It's good for everything: finding the trauma, eliminating resistance, returning to the present... and it's the one thing that most speeds the release of the trauma. The conjunction of that very simple self-love and acceptance, with no strings attached, with feeling the traumatic emotions and body sensations is an incredibly potent mix. People commonly make the mistake of judging themselves for the events in their past. "How could I have done this..." and so on. Or else, they do it at a remove, feeling judgemental but trying to cover it up with excuses. Suspend criticism, suspend judgement, suspend all coping tactics. Love yourself.

White light

White light is how we perceive unobstructed self-awareness. You can temporarily induce a peak state where healing is much easier by pretending that your body, especially your chest, is filled with white light. This light is *you*, and it is *whole*. It might not be healed yet, but it is whole. It also helps to pull in the feeling of a greater presence. Define this 'greater presence' however you wish.

I'd like to clarify that we don't use this light to blast away the trauma or to push it around or to cleanse it or to do anything *to* it. This light is *just there.* You are, for example, feeling this shame in your belly while this bright light of wholeness is just there. [40]

Finding the exact wording of the belief

Often, as a trauma releases, a short phrase, expressing the belief at the core of the trauma, pops into consciousness, sometimes literally bursting out of our mouth. If the trauma doesn't release, it can be helpful to look for this belief. Try different wordings until you hit on the right one (you'll know immediately!) This is especially useful for people whose Centre of Awareness is in their head. The phrase is the mind brain's way to perceive the trauma; the emotion is the heart's; and the physical sensation is the body's. Always try to find the missing piece.

Clearing beliefs about inappropriate emotions

A common block to healing occurs when we shrink from accessing certain emotions, when we think that some emotions are not okay. For example, I saw a woman at a workshop who stayed stuck in a trauma rooted just after her birth. She was feeling a whole mix of emotions and couldn't go any further. We did a little bit of work together and it soon surfaced that she didn't want to feel angry at her mother; she believed that it was not proper for her to feel that. We used the Psychological Reversal step to set aside her objections to feeling anger... and she finally faced the rage. As soon as she did, the incident became clear: she felt herself as a newborn, held upside-down by the delivering doctor. The trauma rapidly released.

Another student was stopped cold by a feeling of evil inside his body. He didn't believe that this was part of a person's normal range of emotions; he thought he'd gone crazy. He pushed the emotions down and became locked in deep depression for a few days. It took surprisingly little help for him to face the 'forbidden' emotion and release the trauma completely.

It's also unsettling to find ourselves experiencing sexual sensations during birth and earlier. The first time I felt this, I shrank away from the feeling, questioning my own sanity. It seemed obscene. I thought I was

---

[40] So far, our observations show that the techniques that use 'psychic' energy, aimed at an injury, do bring about some changes, but that these changes reverse over time. This is because the root cause of the injury has not been addressed.

somehow overlaying adult emotions onto the birth trauma. Reading accounts of such feelings in birth regressions normalized the feeling for me and allowed me to face it. In fact, a certain sensual quality (accompanied by calm, peace and lightness, of course) is a natural part of our body brain's healthy state. And some pre-birth events, conception in particular, are quite sexual in nature.

Sometimes the emotion is a positive one (see 'overlooked traumas' below). The difference between a state of calm, peace and lightness or happiness or love and a 'locked ' positive emotion is our attachment. If you find yourself attached to a certain emotion, defending it or justifying it, it's part of the problem.

Including the other person

A few traumas do not completely release when you just focus on your own experience of them. You have to also be aware of how the other person in the event was affected by what happened, and feel his or her emotions - *without* merging with him or her, of course. This is enough to let the last of the trauma go. (This could simply be because, in those cases, we project some of our own emotions on the other person.) Before birth, emotional mix-ups are especially common because of the nature of our connection to our parents. Checking how your father or mother feels around you also has the advantage of making it obvious if you're copying the other person's emotions. I find that often my emotions, *in utero*, are somewhat similar to my mom's, but they're not exactly the same. I often mistake hers for mine, and the healing stalls. Becoming aware of her presence, and accepting her feelings, solves both problems.

When healing very early and very severe pre-birth traumas, it is sometimes useful to heal the relevant parent first. Try this if you're really stuck: simply expand your awareness - in the past! - to include your mother (or your father, if this is a sperm memory) and heal whatever shows up in your combined bodies - just as with generational traumas, you only need to heal her enough to help yourself; it's easy to get carried away and try to heal all our parents' traumas! - then return to your own body and resume where you left off. The traumas often release faster this way.

Including the other brains, especially the placenta

This is the same principle as above, applied to the multiplicity of your brains. Who are the other characters in what Monti Scribner so aptly calls the soap opera? What do *they* feel about this situation? It's especially easy to forget the placental and spine brains. Your placenta might feel like an envelope all around you—which makes it easy to mistake it for your mother—or a small area around your navel, depending on the moment. Your sperm tail or spine brain, again depending on the moment, can feel envelope-like, draping over your head like a hood and enveloping your lower torso and legs like a sock, or it can feel like a small zone in your mid-back.

Reproducing the body posture

If possible, adopt the posture you seemed to have at the traumatic moment. When healing trauma from a car accident, for example, sit in the position you were in. Find yourself *in utero*? Try the fetal position. Find yourself healing an ancestor who's dying? Lie on the floor in the position he or she seems to be in. If there's a movement that goes with the traumatic moment (for example, hunching forward to avoid the blows of a childhood beating), reproduce that movement as well, gently and in slow motion.

Relaxing your diaphragm, throat and jaw

Tension in the diaphragm is part of the mechanism that locks the dissociated trauma in place. Relaxing the diaphragm helps to reverse this. Loosening the throat and jaw also helps — we do a great deal of holding there, as well. Any bodywork technique can help here, from massaging to gentle stretching, as long as it's not intrusive enough to pull you from regression. Sometimes, though, sitting *with* the tension is what we need to do.

Overlooked Traumas

There are some problems that we're so accustomed to, we think they are just the normal way life works. We take for granted that life is just hard, and that's that. But unless the feeling is accompanied by sensations of calm, peace, and lightness, you're actually running a past trauma. Healing these ingrained, habitual, 'reasonable' emotions can be profoundly life changing. These types of trauma may also be the missing pieces that stall a session. Here are some examples.

Negative emotions for a good reason

Sometimes we overlook troublesome negative emotions because we feel so justified in having them. Take for example intense indignation at the current environmental destruction. One could easily reason that it's important to hang on to this kind of emotion. "If I heal this indignation, will I not stop caring? Won't I end up in disengaged bliss, unwilling to change the situation?" Another example is of someone who needs to hang on to anger because he feels empowered by it. "If I let go, I'll be defenceless." Yet another example is the fear of dying, in someone who actually *is* dying. What can there be to heal, when the feelings are so very appropriate to the situation?

And yet, and yet.

If you are not calm, peaceful and light about something, you are reliving a past trauma. Yes, it's difficult to believe, in these particular cases, but it's still true. Regressing on those types of feelings always reveals a past trauma.[41]

How difficult it is to rock the boat of habitual thinking… What we know is our righteous anger, our defences, our fear. That's the known quantity, the certainty. And what's on the flip side?

Here's Grant again:

> A man contacted me; he was dying of cancer. He'd already lived past the time the doctors gave him, and he was terrified of dying. Since he didn't feel calm, peaceful, and light at the same time as he was terrified, we knew it was something he could heal, although I had my doubts! After all, it seemed so reasonable! It turned out that his fear was actually coming from several incidents in the past, one I recall being a near drowning. Three weeks later he called me up, and said it was the strangest thing — he knew intellectually that he should be afraid, but he wasn't! (In case you're wondering, he survived his cancer.)[42]

---

[41] I've experienced lately what it's like to be indignant about Earth's destruction *while also* being calm peaceful and light… It's very different! There's no 'hook' in it at all.
[42] *The Basic Whole-Hearted Healing Manual*, p. 138.

I know of someone else who only had time for one WHH session before she did die of cancer. All she had time to work on was the fear. Her relatives say the session made a big difference in her last few days.

My defensive-angry friend still cannot be convinced to heal. He's locked in a spiral of depression and would like to get rid of *that*. But when he feels the anger, he feels powerful. Anger is like fireworks, so alive; revenge is sweet. He doesn't realize that the anger and the depression are two sides of the same coin. He doesn't know the power and safety that come from letting go.

And what about political activism? Aren't we at risk of creating a race of blissed-out, disengaged people with this peak state business?

Wait till you see an activist who's in the Beauty Way; they are a wonder to watch. Maybe you already know some: energetic, effective, light-hearted, and absolutely unafraid. They don't get too excited, but they're the ones who bring about the real changes. It's amazing how much energy it takes to maintain righteous indignation. And it's amazing how many wrong targets we can shoot for with trauma-borne anger.

Then there are the ones you'll never see: the ones that are in even better peak states and who quietly work behind the scenes to change the very way humanity thinks. Think, ultimately, about the Dalai Lama. Blissed out? Disengaged?

Positive emotions

Even trickier are the positive emotions that are not accompanied by calm, peace and lightness. The best way to identify them is to spot our attachment to them. Imagine a man who's decided to be forgiving no matter what. What's the difference between him and someone who's in a natural state of forgiveness? Attachment. He just hangs on to that forgiveness whether it's appropriate or not, as if his life depended on it. Sometime in the past, it did. (Isn't that sort of thing easier to spot in someone else than in ourselves, though?)

Those feelings sometimes go with a certain self-image. They creep in on you. For a while everything flows naturally, then a trauma gets triggered and it slides into "Everyone calls me an angel; I'd better cling to whatever angelic feelings I can muster, otherwise they'll abandon me."

Hope, in particular, is a tricky one for me. Whenever I feel hope without the accompanying calm, peace and lightness, it's very difficult for me to examine the feeling. This is because it invariably hides a profound despair.

Grant gives the example of feelings of strength and pride that went with a certain childhood incident. The client acknowledged that these could hide an unreleased emotion. As soon as he approached the feelings in the usual manner, he found that they hid an extreme sense of betrayal. The rest of the childhood event rapidly came into awareness.

Mary tells the story of one of her students who had rapidly progressed to wonderful peak states and advanced healing abilities. One day he showed up or a work session, smiling broadly. "You know, Mary, I think I'm getting addicted to this work." "Uh-oh," Mary replied, jumping immediately into healing mode, "Where in your body is that sense of being addicted to this work?" "No, no, you don't understand, this is a *good* thing. I've never felt so excited in my life!"

It took a lot of convincing to get this student to examine his feelings of excitement and 'being addicted to this good thing'. When he did, it became apparent that he was clinging to them to avoid a dreadful fear of losing his new abilities. The session resulted in... even *better* healing abilities.

Here's how it works: Let's say you are feeling really good - happy, for instance, walking down the street. Then you are hit by a truck! You have a positive emotion at the very onset of the trauma. When the trauma is activated, you feel that emotion. (Some people try to regain that emotion by re-enacting the trauma, and jump in front of trucks.) When healing these traumas, at first you have the positive feelings, but soon enough, you feel the truck.[43]

Healing Physical Problems

Although Whole-Hearted Healing is an emotional healing technique, a surprising number of physical problems respond to it (and to other power therapies as well). There are limits to what it can accomplish, of course. As you read earlier, it definitely won't heal a broken bone; but even there, being calm, peaceful and light while having a broken bone is already a vast improvement. Plus, there's already ample proof from mainstream medicine that improved emotional well-being causes physical injuries to heal faster. One easily-overlooked aspect of doing Whole-Hearted Healing on something like a fracture has to do with the COEX phenomenon: by healing the emotional underpinnings of the injury, one can stop in its tracks a pattern of repeated incidents. There may also be

[43] This wonderful description was kindly provided by Tal.

injuries, such as holes, in the location of the fracture; healing these will also speed up the mending.[44]

Starting from the emotional pain inside the injury

The main strategy is to look for the emotional content of the physical discomfort. Again, we're so very used to avoiding the pain. We ignore it, we medicate it, we do our very best to work around it. Try something new: sink into it until its emotional aspects surface in your consciousness. Then proceed with healing as usual. (And no, you don't have to quit your pain medication to do this. I'm sure you can *remember* the pain well enough!)

A good example of this is Julie's session at the end of Chapter 3. Julie had chronic pain from a head injury and was able to greatly diminish its intensity in just one session. Again, we didn't heal the brain injury, but the improvements to her life were palpable. Julie achieved this simply by sinking into the physical feeling when it arose during the session.

Janov gives an example of a similar approach when he mentions that migraine headaches are a result of birth traumas, and particularly of hypoxia during birth. [45]

Another very powerful trick is to heal the emotions that you feel about the pain or injury itself. For example, you are angry at your body for hurting, or you believe that the pain is proof that you're getting old and useless. Healing this sort of emotions and beliefs often eliminates the physical pain itself. In terms of the triune brains, blaming your body brain for being injured blocks its ability to unite with the rest of you so that you can heal. Instead, it gets stuck in feeling defensive for having been hurt.

---

[44]I wrote the part about fractures from theory, but since then I have put it into practice. I recently encouraged someone to heal the physical pain of a fractured bone while I drove him to hospital for x-rays. It's a long and boring drive from here; he had lots of time. His pain diminished to almost nothing, and there was no swelling! Of course the bone was still broken and displaced, and surgery was still required, but if you've ever broken a bone you will easily imagine the benefits. (The receiving physician commented that he had never seen a fractured cheekbone with no swelling. I just nodded and smiled.)

[45] *The New Primal Scream*, p. 279.

Looking for traumas just before the onset

Sometimes, going into the physical symptoms of an illness, or the emotions about an illness, is not enough. It does bring up some traumas but does not resolve the condition. In these cases, try to find the feelings *just before the condition started.* This is most useful for an illness or injury that has a pattern: a definite start and end, or a clear cycle. You're looking for a moment when some hidden part of you says, 'There it is, here we go again.' Sometimes I wonder how we manage to know about the exact instant, but in my experience people always seem to know just what moment to go for. The next example is most revealing in this respect, because there really didn't seem to be *anything* to work from. Here's the transcript from my notebook:

> We worked on Daniel's dislocated shoulder last night... It's actually a pattern of repeated dislocations, so it doesn't take much physical force for the joint to go out. Of course it's tremendously painful.
>
> I asked him about the very first time it happened. "Nothing was happening, I was just sitting at the kitchen table and I guess I passed out and must have dislocated it when I fell."
>
> Oh dear. What could there be in such a non-event? I had him regress to that moment anyway: sitting at the kitchen table, wife, kids, nothing happening.
>
> So he's just reconstructing that moment. Being himself, just minding his own business, kitchen table wife kids just the usual...
>
> Scanning his body for anything new. Ah: discomfort on top of his head. Sensation of pushing down. Fear and sadness in upper chest...
>
> Birth. Yes. Just like that.
>
> Shoulder pain becomes more intense. Shoulder dystocia?
>
> Maybe not. Sense of a rope under his armpit. What's the movement? Pulled up? Pushed down? Something else?
>
> Pulled up and back. Someone big standing behind him.
>
> A manipulation, doctor's finger under his armpit? But by all indications, his head is still in, maybe crowning. So it would be too early for that.
>
> The cord? The umbilical cord, stuck under his armpit?
>
> "Daniel, merge into the thing under your armpit."
>
> "It's a tube. I'm in a tube."
>
> It's also in front of him. Daniel's visual/tactile cues are peerless. It's just that he doesn't feel much; just gets flashes of what the emotion is.
>
> There's a negotiation taking place, a dilemma between his heart and placenta: injure baby and save cord and placenta, or else preserve baby and injure cord, pinching it or prematurely ripping out the placenta... thereby further injuring baby.

> The moment Daniel succeeds in merging into the entire placenta and amniotic sac, [which, it turns out, was that 'big person' behind him...] the problem completely reframes itself. Placenta is injured too; the 'stuckness' is mutual. It shows up in the placenta's 'shoulder' as well. It's not either/or, it's both. He gets a lot darker with this; it's so desperate. He stays with that overall dark despair until he brightens. We run out of time then, and quit on the win. Outcome: very little pain from then on, no need for painkillers, swift mending. No way to tell yet if the pattern is gone, since Daniel's shoulder only went out every few years.

We use the same principle to mitigate asthma attacks, recurring colds or bouts of influenza, periodic infections and parasites.

This was also the approach I used to heal my back injury, in the example on page 111; I regressed to the moments just before the injury happened. As often, the trauma narrative seems bizarre when juxtaposed with what was happening in my adult life at that moment. I don't know how I remembered the right moment, but I did, and effortlessly. Before that session, I used to injure my lower back quite regularly. It rarely happens now.

Healing our decision to be sick

Sometimes, with the same approach, we find the instant when we *decide to be sick.* This is more difficult to track down, because that decision point can occur long before the illness's onset. Try to remember any very difficult time in the weeks, months or years preceding the illness or injury. Yes, a tall order, but sometimes, as in the examples above, it's easier done than said. Trust your instinct.

Physical illnesses are often 'psychologically reversed,' a term from EFT meaning that our body brain thinks that it must maintain the disease in order to survive. This will manifest in reluctance to get any treatment, and especially in resistance to using power therapies in the cases where the body brain 'knows' these will work. The answer is to use the Psychological Reversal step, as described earlier in this chapter, as often as needed during each session. Try phrases like, "Even though I'm afraid I might die if I heal this, I completely love and accept myself" or "Even though I really don't want to access these feelings, I completely love and accept myself." Use this step on blankness, sleepiness, distraction, inability to concentrate on the healing, and any other obstacle.

After care

After you get improvement in a physical illness or injury, take it easy for a few days. There have been instances where injured joints or soft-tissue injuries suddenly became painless, but still needed the usual amount of time to fully heal. And just as with psychological conditions, please ask the prescribing physician for a reassessment before quitting your medication! Quitting antibiotics before taking the full course can be particularly hazardous.

Chapter 6

Integrating Other Techniques

Whole-Hearted Healing doesn't have to exist in a vacuum. You can successfully combine it with many other healing techniques, and get better results than with each one separately. You can speed up WHH and lessen its physical discomfort by boosting it with an energy therapy; use the principles of it to deepen the results of other regression modalities; or take advantage of a bodyworker's willing and experienced hands to propel yourself into a comprehensive healing experience.

TAT, EFT, and Other 'Energy Therapies'

Our Institute uses EFT, the most widely used meridian therapy, as one of its bread-and-butter healing techniques. We use it for all kinds of applications. It's not my place to teach it here, but you can go to Gary Craig's website, emofree.com, and find a free tutorial. (For those already familiar with it, there is also a one-page synopsis in appendix C.) Although there are many subtleties in EFT's application, the basics are easy to learn.

A host of other meridian therapies exist; they all work on the same principles.

Strangely enough, nobody yet knows exactly *how* they work; our experiments have shown that the mechanism is different from WHH; meridian therapies seem to dissolve the structures that hold the traumas in place at the cellular level, rather than acting directly on the traumas. The effect is somewhat gentler.

TAT, the Tapas Acupressure Technique, is a bit different. We're not sure exactly how it works either, but somehow it seems to heal generational traumas easily, something EFT doesn't do well. The impression, as the trauma releases, is the same as with meridian therapies: the emotions seem to simply dissolve, rather than let go with the attendant sensation of shifting energy or emotional release, as in Whole-Hearted Healing. TAT seems to work best on people who have at least some degree of Underlying Happiness (the peak state involving fusion of the body and heart brains). We don't know if it's reversible, something that occasionally happens with EFT.[46]

The trouble with meridian techniques applied on their own is that they don't give you a clear view of past traumas as a cause of the problem you want to heal. Thus, trouble shooting, solely from an energy therapy point of view, doesn't necessarily yield the necessary insights to solve the problem. Adding the insights from regression can drastically speed up and deepen the healing, and it also helps you understand and integrate the interesting transpersonal experiences that pop up along the way.[47]

On the other hand, Whole-Hearted Healing is slower (for most people, anyway; I can now heal faster with it than one could with EFT, and some of my students, possibly because they start off with good peak states, can release traumas in seconds right from their first session). Some people experience significant physical pain while they regress, which would

---

[46] Grant and his students have done a number of experiments on how and why EFT sometimes reverses. Reversals involve stressed, 'unnatural' breathing accompanied by the emotional tone of the original trauma. See *The Basic Whole-Hearted Healing Manual*, p. 124-125, for details.

And a footnote to this footnote... Grant added this to my manuscript: "*Meridian therapies can be reversed because the entire trauma structure hasn't been eliminated, just the trauma that is giving the current symptoms. To make the healing irreversible, one has to be sure that the entire trauma string has been fully eliminated. We've found that using just the gamut point is an easy way to do this, as it appears to address the entire trauma structure, not just the presenting trauma moment.*"

[47] It's also worth noting that energy therapies don't work on everyone. EFT doesn't work on me, which is why I know so much about WHH! I find that about 25% of my students end up discarding EFT as unsatisfactory. I'm sure that a more experienced practitioner would have better success rates.

certainly make Whole-Hearted Healing unpalatable as a long-term healing modality.

One way to overcome the limitations of each approach is to use a hybrid of both. To do this, use the WHH format for regression. Once you're in the past and you feel both the emotion *and* body sensation clearly, instead of just waiting the trauma out, aim your meridian therapy at *both*. Many things happen then:

-By aiming your healing at both the body sensation and the emotion (and at the worded belief, if you know what it is), you heal several aspects of the trauma at once, instead of having to chase after the different aspects from the present.

-By regressing, then healing from your point of view in the past, you reach further down the 'string' before applying the meridian therapy, and this achieves a more wide-ranging result. This, again, takes care of more aspects of the trauma in one go.

-By staying in your body in the past, you make sure that you'll feel all the relevant emotions and body sensations, and you get to heal each brain's contribution to the trauma. You're also more likely to spot archetypal images and all the other tricky ways we have to dissociate from parts of ourselves. Meridian therapies will not release 'copied' traumas. If you regress, you can spot copies in the usual way (most likely because you'll have done a few rounds of tapping with no changes), then ask yourself what your own emotions are, then continue with your meridian therapy on your own emotions.

The main reason we always teach Whole-Hearted Healing before any advanced healing technique, regardless of the students' peak states, is that if anything blocks or fails with the faster techniques, they can always return to WHH, if only for a few minutes, until they've solved their problem. This is also applicable with energy therapies. If any trauma fails to release with your energy therapy, just use WHH until you have cleared the hurdle. This is particularly likely to happen with generational traumas, copies and holes.

For safety reasons, you should use a healing modality that cannot reverse itself (WHH, Traumatic Incident Reduction or any technique that involves regression, rather than a meridian therapy) whenever you heal any trauma that makes you feel suicidal.

Exercise: Healing with a hybrid of EFT and WHH

I'm using EFT as the modality here, but of course you can substitute any energy therapy. You'll find that most of the steps are identical to the basic WHH steps in Chapter 1.

Step 1: Start with something that's bothering you in the present, just as with the basic technique. Get yourself worked up about it. Write down how you feel, and a few words about what makes you feel that way.

Step 2: Magnify the emotion if you can. Where does it sit in your body? Or: if you are starting from a body sensation, magnify that. What's the emotion inside it?

Step 3: Recall other times when you felt exactly this way. It won't necessarily be the same kind of incident: you're looking for the same type of emotion and body sensation. Choose the earliest incident you can recall, even if it doesn't seem to make logical sense.

Step 4: Place your hand on your chest to remind yourself to stay inside your body. (Yes, it's just as important to be in your body, to make sure you heal your emotions *in the past* rather than just *about the past.*) If you see yourself 'out there', merge with the image of yourself until there's only one 'you'. This is the most important step. If this is difficult, try the 'Loving Yourself' technique. Bring the image to yourself and put it on like a sweater. Relaxing your diaphragm, throat and jaw also helps.

Step 5: Love yourself in this moment in the past. Stay in the moment, feeling the emotion and the body sensations. As soon as you feel both clearly, start doing EFT on *both* the emotion and body sensation. (For example: "Even though I have this tightness and fear in my chest, I completely love and accept myself...")[48]

---

[48] It is common to take shortcuts when doing EFT as a hybrid with WHH. Many people find that they can omit the Psychological Reversal step. If the healing stalls, though, make sure to include it for a round or two. *Always* include it if you're treating anything related to addictions or any conditions your body might be attached to. Most

Step 6: Reassess how you feel in this moment in the past. There may be other emotions and body sensations to heal. Or you might spontaneously move to an earlier trauma. Use EFT on each component of the trauma. There most likely will be several. The earliest prebirth memory always involves a physical injury, so make sure to pay attention to body sensations.

Step 7: When nothing is left except calm, peace and lightness, you are done. If the moment you healed is before birth, you should also feel large and bright. Stay in the moment for a few minutes, to make sure no further trauma arises. If one does, go back to Step 4.

Step 8: Check your work. There should be no out-of-body image when you look back at the traumatic moment. Look at the description you wrote at the start of the process. It should no longer trigger you. If any emotions besides calm, peace and lightness are present, return to Step 4 or plan to return at a later session.

Other Regression Techniques

You can enhance any other regression technique by adding Whole-Hearted Healing's key features: *stay in your body* and *keep healing long enough to reach and heal the earliest trauma.* Apart from these principles, the main differences between various regression therapies lie in the induction methods used to access the past, and in the expectations about how far back in the past is enough. By all means use your favourite, or combine it with the simple regression method of Whole-Hearted Healing. But make sure to stay in your body in the past, and to integrate whatever comes up—be it a projection, a pretend-identity, an archetypal image, or any of the other ways we dissociate from parts of ourselves. You will find the results much more reliable. Remember also that the end

---

people also omit the 'nine gamut procedure,' confining themselves to the tapping sequence. As you saw in footnote 44, Grant and his student only use the gamut point in most cases. If the shortcuts don't work, return to the whole routine.

point of healing is a feeling of calm, peace and lightness about your issue. Do not settle for mere reframing or intellectual understanding.

I recently started working with a very courageous woman who has chosen to tackle issues of early childhood abuse through regression. She had already tried several types of regression techniques before she inquired about Whole-Hearted Healing. This was her comment after our first session together: "This is the only regression work I've ever done that does not leave me feeling traumatized." She explained that with the other techniques she had tried, she had always viewed the trauma moments from outside her body, like a movie 'out there', and that it always felt like the session itself re-traumatized her. She added, "I find that when I merge with the image of myself, the emotions actually become more gentle."

One of the Australian schools of breathwork, Nemi Nath's BreathConnection, has recently started integrating our Institute's methods with their own. An enthusiastic collaboration is now in progress. This is of great benefit to all of us, given breathwork's longer history and our own Institute's understanding of peak states and transpersonal experiences.

Bodywork

Again, bodywork is an excellent way to access traumas, and speeds up their release as well. Unfortunately, I know of few people who have exploited this fully. Some of our advanced therapists do combine bodywork with our advanced techniques, which allow 'hands-off' release of traumas, but few people - except for Grant, in the early days of developing this technique - have played with *receiving* a bodywork treatment while doing WHH on themselves. This section, then, is necessarily self-referential...

So far, I've combined Whole-Hearted Healing with reiki, massage, acupuncture, Rolfing, shiatsu and cranio-sacral therapy. In each instance, I've let the therapist know at the outset that I would be doing my own regression process during the session, and warned him or her that I sometimes get rather emotional while doing this and that I took entire responsibility for my own welfare. I have never yet encountered any resistance to this.

At the start of the session, I talk about the issues I'm trying to heal, just as I would in a normal session. The therapist asks questions, I clarify, we do the usual intake process.

During the session, I simply work on whatever comes up. Emotions and images arise vividly. I rarely know what they mean, but that doesn't matter. I use them as metaphors, and stay in my body and love myself and just heal. Generational traumas, in particular, seem to be stored deep in my tissues. The bodywork both brings them to awareness and hastens their release.

Since release always translates into a shift in body tension, the therapist, in my experience, always senses it accurately and moves on to the next area at exactly the right time. Different aspects of a trauma get stored in various areas of the body. By the time the session is complete, every stone has been turned.

Sometimes the communication style of the therapist has to be slightly adapted to the regression style. Partway into my very first cranio-sacral session, the therapist, already aware of my work, said, "At this point, it is customary to speak to the injury." I simply replied, "If that's all right, I will speak *as* the injury instead."

That was the only adjustment needed. At the end of the session, slightly concerned about whether my methods were a disruption, I asked how it had gone for him. "Often," he said rather mournfully, "doing cranio-sacral therapy is like dragging heavy furniture across a rough cement floor." (*Now you've done it*, I told myself.) He broke into a wide smile. "This was like using one finger to push around furniture, on perfectly-oiled casters, across a polished floor."

One of Grant's students, who has since gone on to other things, suggested using acupressure with Whole-Hearted Healing. As homework after a telephone session, he told me to find all the pressure points in a given area of my body, work each one in turn, and heal any trauma arising. I later experimented some more with the technique, looking up in a book the pressure points corresponding to a certain physical ailment. My results were startling. I found that for almost every point, there might be one trauma arising from shallow pressure, a second one from deep pressure, and, most unexpected, a third and sometimes a fourth arising from gradual *release* of the pressure. I simply maintained whatever pressure triggered the trauma, healed the emotions and body sensations, then moved on to the next stage.

This certainly could use further exploration, but here's my provisional method (with apologies to the therapists with the real training). Try it once you're feeling comfortable with WHH and can release traumas quickly. Or else invent your own adaptation.

Exercise: Using WHH with acupressure or reflexology (solo method)

1) Find the pressure points relevant to the problem you want to work on, using any of the piles of great books on the subject, or by consulting with your favourite therapist.

2) Apply slight pressure on the first point. Gradually increase the pressure until a trauma image or sensation appears, anywhere in your body.

3) Do WHH on the arising trauma.

4) Increase the pressure until the next trauma sensation or image appears. Heal that.

5) Continue working the point until no more traumas arise.

6) Very gradually, release the pressure. If another trauma appears, stop, maintain the same amount of pressure, and heal the trauma.

7) Continue gradually releasing the pressure, stopping to release anything else that arises.

8) Move on to the next point.

And Onwards...

There are all sorts of other possibilities for combining therapies. Grant mentions using meditation as a method to spot traumas, and using visualisation and affirmations, not in the conventional way but as a way to unearth, and thus make available for healing, your resistance to what you want in your life. Others are combining Whole-Hearted Healing with yoga, or with techniques from shamanic traditions.

Whole-Hearted Healing might be something you only use to resolve a few problems, then store in the emergency cupboard of your mind, along with the candles and the first aid kit... Or it can become a regular practice, an attitude you integrate with everything in your life, a new way of feeling, of exploring, of being.

Hornby Island, B.C., February 2012

Appendix A

Healing Resistance to Using the Loving-Yourself Technique

Try this exercise, after you have gained your sea legs with WHH, if you still have trouble using the Loving-Yourself technique as it is explained in Chapter 2. As long as you haven't healed the problem, it is perfectly all right to use different, less-threatening concepts, such as 'accepting and honouring yourself', instead of 'loving yourself', to speed up the release of the traumas.

Unblocking your ability to use this little technique can also open up all sorts of wondrous and dangerous-seeming things having to do with self-love... It's well worth the effort.

There is an example of the use of this method at the end of Chapter 3.

1) Attempt to do the 'Loving Yourself' exercise from Chapter 2. How far along can you make it? At the point where the difficulty arises, ask yourself, What's in the way?

2) Magnify whatever it is that's in the way. Do the usual healing on it: what's the emotion of it? Where is that resistance sitting in your body? Heal that with WHH or EFT, whichever works best for you.

3) Attempt again to do the Loving-Yourself exercise. If you still can't, ask yourself, What's in the way now?

4) Again focus on what's in the way. Don't judge yourself, just honour and accept yourself for having that resistance. Heal it just as you did for the previous obstacle.

5) Continue cycles of trying the Loving-Yourself exercise and healing the resistance that shows up, until you can do the exercise effortlessly.

Appendix B

Healing Resistance to Moving your Centre of Awareness

Try this exercise, after you have gained a certain level of comfort with WHH, if you still have trouble moving your Centre of Awareness (CoA) as explained in Chapter 2. It is very important to heal this if you intend to use WHH long term, as gaining full access to all your brains is necessary to unblock all those wonderful fusion peak states. As long as you haven't healed the problem, it is perfectly all right to use the slightly less threatening approach of 'putting your attention on' various parts of your body, but truly feeling from inside will make your healings much more effective.

There are often very big traumas blocking full access. Simply put, if you can't move your CoA to your lower belly, for example, it is either because 'you' are very worried about what you might find there, or because your body brain, residing in your lower belly, is worried about being seen. Expect this healing to take a few sessions, especially if your CoA is completely immobile. If you can already move it in a limited way, it means you have less severe traumas.

It would be helpful to review the sections on archetypes and pretend-identities in Chapter 4 before attempting this. You are very likely to encounter some of those (body brain as swamp monster or ghost of Hitler reborn, etc.) as your brains start relaxing their resistance to being seen and felt.

Expect some very strange dreams while you're on this healing project. Remember, the characters in your dreams are all aspects of yourself. Use the emotional content of those dreams to further your work

1) Locate your Centre of Awareness. Where is it? How big is it? Record your starting point in your notebook; we do tend to forget and to undervalue our progress.

2) Attempt to move your CoA, following the exercise in Chapter 2, but this time try to move it to the seat of the different brains: your crown brain just above your head, your mind inside your head, your heart in your chest, your solar plexus, your body brain in your lower belly. Go slowly; experiment with touching gently the target area; just try to sense from within each area.

3) Note which areas you can access and which you have trouble with. Is your CoA completely stationary, or can it move to some of the brains?

4) Start with just one brain that you can't access. If there is more than one, start with the one you most wish to access right now.

5) Check yourself for any prejudices *about* that brain (for example, 'if I access my crown brain, I might become one of those flaky spiritual people I dislike so much'). Start by healing these prejudices, from the point of view of your CoA in its present location. Use EFT or WHH, whichever one works best for you.

6) Now attempt to move your CoA to the brain you're trying to access: try to feel from inside it. What's in the way?

7) Magnify whatever it is that's in the way. Do the usual healing on it: what's the emotion of it? Where is that resistance sitting in your body? Heal that with WHH or an energy therapy.

8) Attempt again to feel from inside the brain you're trying to access. If you still can't, ask yourself, What's in the way now?

9) Again focus on what's in the way. Don't judge yourself, just love yourself for having that resistance. Heal it just as you did for the previous obstacle.

10) Continue cycles of trying to feel from your target brain and healing the resistance that shows up. Please have patience with yourself; these are often very big traumas. It's time well spent to heal this, because it will facilitate your access to all kinds of peak states.

11) Once you have regained access to one renegade brain, congratulate yourself profusely. Then, perhaps in a different session, redo the process for any other brain to which you can't move your CoA. Don't forget your placenta (in your navel as an adult) and your spine brain (in the middle of your back). Give a try to feeling from your perineum and third eye as well. What do *they* have to say?

Appendix C: EFT in Brief

From Gary Craig, (www.emofree.com). This site offers more information on EFT, including a free downloadable manual (video training DVDs are available for purchase).

<u>THE SETUP:</u> Repeat 3 times…this affirmation:
"Even though I **have** this……? (or Even though I **still have** some of this……?) I deeply and completely accept myself." (The Reminder Phrase is just one or two words from your affirmation)

While continuously rubbing the Sore Spot,
or tapping the karate chop point.

<u>THE SEQUENCE</u>: Tap about <u>7 times</u> on each of the following energy points while repeating the Reminder Phrase at each point.

EB = Beginning of the eyebrow
SE = Side of the Eye
UE = Under the Eye
UN = Under the Nose
Ch = Chin
CB = Beginning of the collarbone
UA = Under the Arm
Th = Thumb
IF = Index Finger
MF = Middle Finger
BF = Baby Finger
KC = Karate Chop

FIRST THIRD FIFTH SEVENTH

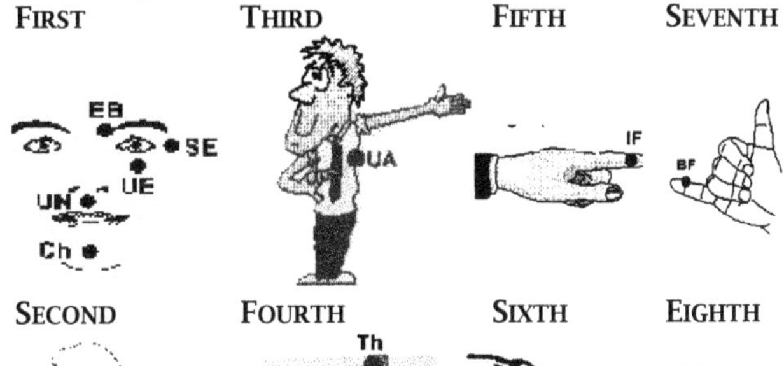

SECOND FOURTH SIXTH EIGHTH

CB Th MF KC

<u>**The 9 Gamut Procedure:**</u>
Continuously tap on the Gamut point while performing each of these 9 actions: (The Gamut point is on the back of the hand, between the pinkie and ring finger tendons.)

1. Eyes closed	**2. Eyes open**	**3. Eyes hard down right**
4. Eyes hard down left	**5. Roll eyes in circle**	**6. Roll eyes in the other direction**
7. Hum 2 seconds of a song	**8. Count to 5**	**9. Hum 2 seconds of a song**

<u>THE SEQUENCE (again)</u>: Tap about <u>7 times</u> on each of the following energy points while repeating the Reminder Phrase at each point.

EB, SE, UE, UN, Ch, CB, UA, Th, IF, MF, BF, KC

NOTE: In each subsequent round, the **Setup Affirmation** and the **Reminder Phrase** is adjusted to reflect that you are addressing the <u>**remaining**</u> problem.

Appendix D

A Field Guide to Special Situations

Special situations in healing are just that: special. Ninety percent of your healing will be regular traumas.

People get mixed up between all the different Special Situations and I can't blame them: there's nearly two dozen of them (depending what you include) and you only see them rarely - you will probably never see them all unless you're a therapist.

I propose here a system that might take us closer to the goal of missing nothing and keeping sessions going and having a reasonable idea of what's going on, regardless of our own state of consciousness; for example, it's easy to see a generational string if you have great 'seeing', and to tell it apart from an archetype, but if you're working blind it's not that obvious sometimes. This document assumes that you're working from average consciousness, with average perceptions.

This approach groups special instances by some of their experiential characteristics. This does *not* mean that these phenomena are from similar *causes.* But it's one way to remember the damn things and to narrow down the problems in the fire of the action.

This chart is similar to a key in a botany book: it will help you identify your strange specimen, but it won't tell you how to treat it. Refer back to the chapters on special situations - Chapter 1 for the short version and chapter 4 for the more detailed - for help in healing the problem.

Sometimes it's simply not clear. Fortunately, several problems are treated the same way (for example, if it's something outside you, you almost always merge with it and see what happens next). At other times you just have to try out different things (for example, "let's see what happens if we construe this as a copy"). If the healing doesn't get unstuck, well, you try something else.

To heal a trauma with a regression therapy, you have to be inside your body, inside the trauma, in the past. And really, this is about spotting and remedying the tricky ways we have of not being in-body, of avoiding the core of the trauma: we hide it in a hole, shroud it in numbness, project it onto some scary being out there, mask it with someone else's emotions, fail to see it as extending up our genetic line... So this is still basic WHH, and it's still about being inside the trauma in the past, and about welcoming home these lost bits of ourselves.

Spotting and managing special situations during sessions

Special instances can show up at three different times:

1. At the outset, as we approach the issue:
2. During the session;
3. At the session's end.

Problems that show up as we approach the issue

Some special instances will show up right off the bat. Please remember that *all* of them may also show up later in a session.

They are:

- **Dilemmas**. Your initial problem seems like an insoluble dilemma, often corresponding to a pair of opposites. The dilemma position may lead to all kinds of traumas but it may return as earlier versions of itself later on in the session.

- **Projection**. Your initial problem seems to be mainly about another person's behaviour.

- **Soul pieces**. Your problem is associated with voices or noise in your mind; or you want to heal an inability to concentrate, or related problems. Soul pieces may be part of the problem with addictions.

- **Emptiness or holes** *could* theoretically show up as part of your initial problem. **Soul loss** as well, I suppose. But holes usually hide behind all sorts of resistance and you're much more likely to see them after the session gets under way.

- I suppose **past lives,** the access to one of them, could also show up as a problem someone would want to heal. Uncontrollable access to past lives would show up as a spiritual emergency. Or you might want to heal a habit of taking refuge in past lives to avoid present problems.

- **Generational traumas** are an interesting one. As one starts a healing session, one can often spot the *likelihood* of a generational trauma: the problem seems terribly personal or feels like the very core of who you are; or there is an obvious history of the same problem happening to others in your family. But the generational string itself is unlikely to appear until later in the session. If there is a *clear* history, you can induce access to the generational string by thinking back to the furthest relative who might have had the problem, often a grandparent or great-grand. Some people will immediately perceive the rest of the string, others need to stay merged with that relative for a while, healing arising sensations, before the string completes itself.

  Note that it could be unsafe to merge into a living relative from the present (because of the soul-stealing problem) -- but there have been no problems with merging with close relatives (parents, aunts, grandparents) from within a regressed state - probably because what we're actually merging with is our own genetic material.

- **Vortices** may happen with addictions, and I also saw them in a client who came in complaining of depression. Whenever you focus on your problem, you get a spinning sensation or even see a tornado or vortex. Or your chief complaint itself is a spinning dizziness whose medical causes have been ruled out.

Problems that show up while in session

This is when we start looking at flowcharts.
You know there's a special instance going on when:

A. You perceive something that doesn't fit the profile of a regular trauma, or;
B. The healing stalls.

You perceive something that doesn't fit the profile of a regular trauma

Isn't that simple: accept whatever you perceive - tactilely, visually, or any other way. It's weird? Fine. Be open to the idea that this session might not be exactly what you intended it to be.

Many of these situations are remedied by merging with whatever special new thing shows up, so that's a good broad category to remember. Then there's Table 1 and Table 2 (next two pages):

Table 1

You feel something **inside** your body, that does not fit the profile of a regular trauma.			
⇓ **new pain** or other sharp physical sensation ⇓ does it have a definite shape? ⇓ if yes, could also be a **structure**. If in doubt treat as "new pain"	⇓ a sense of being someone or something else ⇓ **pretend-identity, archetype, past life**, could be a **generational trauma** in rare cases; could also be a **structure**. In all cases you start off by merging and accepting until the situation clarifies itself.	⇓ an emotion seeming to belong to someone else ⇓ **copy**, in most cases. If it doesn't release, try treating as a **soul piece**.	⇓ movement ⇓ If spinning: **vortex**. Otherwise, give in to movement anyway and treat as **regular trauma.**

Table 2

<table>
<tr><td colspan="4">You feel something outside your body.</td></tr>
<tr><td>⇓
ancestor(s):
one or many?</td><td></td><td rowspan="2">⇓
other being or shape
⇓
archetype, projection, soul pieces. It could also be a placental trauma. Treat soul pieces by Silent Mind Technique; merge with everything else.</td><td rowspan="2">⇓
movement
⇓
spinning: big vortex, or passage through swirling fluid? Give in to the movement until situation clarifies.

Any other movement: give in to movement and treat as regular trauma.</td></tr>
<tr><td>⇓
one: merge and reassess for perception of others beyond him. If there's still only one, heal him. Others sometimes show up later.</td><td>⇓
many: if sequential, go to earliest / furthest away, merge and heal

If they're a group of contemporaries, merge with group, centering on leader. (I think this is a case of getting to the bottom of a vortex without feeling the spinning.)</td></tr>
<tr><td colspan="4">Other unusual situation, not fitting above descriptions:</td></tr>
<tr><td>⇓
Situation blamed on other person: projection</td><td>⇓
Insoluble dilemma</td><td>⇓
treat all other situations as regular trauma; keep an open mind for other possibilities.</td><td></td></tr>
</table>

The healing stalls

If the healing stalls, *it means a piece of the puzzle is missing.* The 3 main types of puzzle pieces are:

1. **You are missing a sensation that is inside your body**. Most often it is that you forget that the *absence* of feeling is, itself, a feeling. So check for blankness and lack. These most often hide **emptiness** or a **hole**, but there can be **soul loss**. Without advanced sight, I'd say treat as emptiness/hole, which is the most common problem, and if you get nowhere try the soul loss cure. Keep in mind that some people need to heal a lot of resistance before they'll dare feel a hole. In the process of checking or healing blankness, you might start feeling something else in your body and you're back at **Table 1**. Another type of missing sensation happens when you're **overlooking** a trauma: **"positive" emotions** with a component of attachment are the trickiest. See chapter 5.

2. **You are stuck in an emotion that is copied** from someone. This is simple to check for, so it's worth spending the time. Feel into the area right around your body. Could the emotion (or even the body sensation) belong to someone just outside?

3. **You are missing something that is outside your body.** Even if the answer to 2 is negative, you've started to pay attention to your surroundings. Continue this for a while; you might come up with a sense of **something outside**, even just a modification of colour or weight. Then you're back to **table 2**. If you're not sure what the outside thing is, just merge with it until the situation clarifies.

Ok, so let's make a third table to sum up the trouble shooting of stalled sessions:

Table 3

The session stalls when a piece of the puzzle is missing. 1. Check **inside**:			
⇓ emptiness or lack? ⇓ If yes: - **Emptiness** - **Hole** - **Soul loss** (rarely)	⇒if no, any **overlooked traumas**? ⇓ **positive emotions**, etc.	⇒ if no, any new sensations inside? ⇓ if yes, go to **table 1.**	⇒ if no, gently feel into the area immediately around you... ⇓ ⇓
⇒2. Check **outside**:			
	⇒ if no: continue feeling around outside. Pay attention to any new perception. ⇓ **Table 2**	⇒ if no results: check **externals.** ⇓ **resistance from your other brains.** ⇓ **interference from another person in the present** (use projection technique on your relationship with this person).	⇒ Then start over where you left off!

Problems that show up at the end of the session

The main problem here could be **soul loss**. Then there's the problem that's not a problem: a **transpersonal experience** or a new **peak state**. (Check for resistance to the new sensations.) Otherwise, go back to the top, because you're starting another cycle!

Appendix E

Trouble-Shooting Guide

About Using the Basic Technique

I'm not sure if my medication will prevent me from regressing...

See '*Medications*' page 21.

I can't stay in my body...

First see page 131, *'Psychological Reversal Step'*. Also see page 39 (the various tricks for moving your CoA might work to put you in-body).

I can't feel emotions...

First see pages 61 and 122; if the problem is temporary, check the sections on '*Blankness*' on page 79, '*Overlooked emotions*' on page 138 and '*Prejudice about what the trauma might be*' on page 124.

I'm not able to love myself...

See page 37, the example on page 71 and *Appendix A*.

I keep feeling distracted when I try to heal...

See '*Prejudice about what the trauma might be*', page 124, '*Distraction from a bigger trauma*', page 124, and the '*Psychological Reversal Step*' on page 131.

Whenever I try to focus on my issue, I feel very sleepy...

See '*New physical pain*', page 83, and the '*Psychological Reversal Step*', page 131.

I get a jumble of sensations but cannot tell where I've regressed to, or if I've regressed at all...

See the notes under '*Step 6*', starting on page 67; also the '*Image Streaming process*' on page 134.

I get images, but they don't look like anything I know...

Same references as above, plus the example in the section on '*Blankness*', page 79.

I'm afraid of what could happen if I let my anger out...

See '*Good news for those of us who live in small apartments*' page 73, and also '*Clearing beliefs about inappropriate emotions*,' page 136. Then bite the bullet and read '*Considering the worst-case scenario*,' page 125.

I don't want to experience the physical discomfort of regression...

See page 147. Also, make sure you're completely in-body... And see the example under '*Other regression techniques*' on page 151.

About Presenting Problems

The problem isn't mine; it's my wife's, and she doesn't want to do this healing thing...

Sorry... See '*Projections*' on page 105.

I keep hearing my mother's voice criticizing me...

See '*Soul stealing*', page 86. If that's not what it is, treat like '*Recurring music*', page 127.

I think I'm channelling weird stuff from someone else...

See '*Soul stealing*', page 86.

My problem is physical, and this is an emotional healing technique...

See '*Healing physical problems*', page 141.

I have a physical problem I'd like to heal, but I keep forgetting to work on it...

See '*Using the Psychological Reversal Step*, page 131.

I'm sure my problem is karmic...

See '*Past lives*', page 101.

I'm trying to stop smoking...

See the footnote on page 99.

I had this horrible nightmare...

See '*Archetypal images*' page 92, and '*Dreams*', page 127.

About Special Situations in Healing

(see also the flowcharts in Appendix D)

I saw this big scary black hole...

See '*Holes*', page 80.

I sense the devil right in front of me!..

See '*Archetypal images*', page 92.

I feel blank...

See '*Emptiness and blank feeling*,' page 79.

I feel a crawly, shivery sensation on part of my skin...
See '*Holes*,' page 80. Otherwise, heal like normal trauma.

I feel this horrible emptiness...
See '*Emptiness*' and '*Holes*', page 79.

The healing is making my chronic pain worse...
See '*New physical pain*,' page 83.

The healing is causing some new physical pain...
Same reference as above.

I'm pretty sure my issue is gone, but I feel bleak and flat...
See '*Soul loss*', page 90; but see also the example on page 86.

The emotions are too overwhelming...
See '*Psychological Reversal Step*', page 131.

I'm presented with an impossible choice, so I don't even know what I should heal...
See '*Dilemmas*', page 110.

I sort of feel like God, and I'm sure this is a terrible sin or sacrilege...
See '*Transpersonal Experiences and Peak States*', page 115.

I feel sexual feelings while I'm inside my mother; I worry that I must be some kind of pervert...
See '*Clearing Beliefs about Inappropriate Emotions*' page 136.

I feel like I'm really evil; I worry that I've gone mad...
See the section on '*Holes*' from page 80, including the case example at the end of the section. Also see '*Archetypal Images*,' page 92.

I took a nap after my unfinished session and woke up feeling very dizzy...
See '*Vortices*', page 98.

I healed something and felt this beautiful feeling of unity, then it went away and I feel a huge sense of loss...

See '*Transpersonal Experiences and Peak States*', page 115.

I sense a solid object, like an implant, inside me...

See '*Structures*', page 114.

I see what looks like a past life, and I don't even believe in those!...

See '*Past Lives*', page 101.

I've got a big trauma that is unresolved, I feel terrible and I have to go to work for 3 days and there's no time to heal right now...

See '*No Time to Finish*', page 119; see also the section on *Energy Therapies*, starting on page 147. (You can use energy therapies, without regression, to heal discomfort on the fly.)

I've sat with these emotions and body sensations for half an hour and nothing's changed...

Start with '*Copies*', page 83; see also the different headings under '*Difficulties in Releasing the Trauma*', page 134, and '*Overlooked Traumas*', page 138.

I'm trying to focus on this one big problem and keep being distracted by side issues...

See '*Distraction from a Bigger Trauma,*' page 124; also see the '*Psychological Reversal Step'*, page 131.

I'm willing to heal anything, but I *don't* want to touch [issue X]...

Uh-oh. See '*Considering the Worst-Case Scenario*' on page 125, with the attached warning in the footnote, and decide whether WHH really is an appropriate technique for you after all.

I have a piece of music stuck in my head, and it's distracting me from healing...

See '*Music*', page 127; you could also try treating it as a '*Soul Piece*', page 86.

I feel a jumble of emotions and sensations and I don't know where to start...

See under '*New Physical Pain*', page 83; check also the '*Strategies for accessing traumas'*, page 122.

I only have these vague sensations and I can't pinpoint where they come from...

Start with '*Scanning your Body*', page 133. You may also have to use the '*Psychological Reversal Step'*, page 131.

I'm not calm, peaceful and light, but the emotion that is left is one that I consider necessary (for my survival, my life-task, my integrity, or my well-being)...

See '*Overlooked Traumas*', page 138.

About Learning WHH in the Context of Long-Term Training with our Institute

I don't understand why I have to learn this basic technique when I already have the peak states required for advanced healing...

See Grant's *Foreword* on page 10; also see the discussion about integrating various therapies in *Chapter 6*, especially page 149.

I don't understand why I shouldn't merge with my clients...

See '*Soul Stealing*', starting on page 86, right to the end of the section.

I'm used to cleansing injuries with light and I'd like to combine that with WHH...

See '*White Light*', page 135; also see the example on page 82.

I'm a therapist who uses other healing modalities and I'd like to combine that with WHH...

See *Chapter 6* for some starting ideas.

Appendix F

Resources

Spiritual Emergencies

Canada

Spiritual Emergence Service

A free service, organized along the guidelines set by Dr. Stanislav and Christina Grof. Volunteers can answer questions about any psycho-spiritual difficulties and provide you a free referral to a therapist in your area. There is also an extensive list of therapists for self-referral. The website now includes links to spiritual emergency services in 28 countries.

www.spiritualemergence.net/pages/ home.html
Telephone: +1 (604) 533-3545

USA

Spiritual Emergence Network

The newly-rebuilt website offers a list of therapists all over the US for self-referral; it can also handle on-line information requests.

www.cpsh.org

Australia

Spiritual Emergence Network Australia

www.spiritualemergence.org.au/index.html

United Kingdom

Spiritual Crisis Network

The site offers information and links to crisis lines and therapists' associations, but has no direct referral service.

www.spiritualcrisisnetwork.org.uk/index.htm

Books

There are also some excellent books about spiritual emergence/ emergency. Most notably:

- Emma Bragdon, *The Call of Spiritual Emergency.* San Francisco: Harper and Row, 1990, 243 pp.
- Emma Bragdon, *A Sourcebook for Helping People in Spiritual Emergency,* Lightening Up Press, California, 1988.
- Grof, Stanislav, MD, and Christina Grof: *Spiritual Emergency.* Los Angeles: J. P. Tarcher, 1989.

For therapists and anyone who's interested in using power therapies long term, we highly recommend the online course on spiritual emergencies by Dr David Lukoff at spiritual-emergency.com/dsm4/course_dsmiv.asp. This course is part of our requirements for certification as a peak state therapist.

Suicide Prevention

Metanoia

Educational material and resources for immediate help via e-mail or phone. This service is geared for North America, but the website is very direct and has some excellent information, for people in crisis, but also for those who help them. They also offer what certainly looks like useful, non-judgemental support, by volunteers, via email.

www.metanoia.org/suicide/

Canada-wide

The Centre for Suicide Prevention

A listing of crisis centres across the country.

www.suicideinfo.ca

British Columbia

Crisis Intervention and Suicide Prevention Centre of British Columbia.

Provides education about suicide and resources. The emergency help line number is 1 800 784-2433 (1 800 SUICIDE)

www.crisiscentre.bc.ca

United States

National Suicide Prevention Hotline

Telephone: +1 (800) SUICIDE

Outside North America

Most countries have national crisis/suicide help lines… find out how to contact them *before* you need them!

Other Power Therapies

EFT (Emotional Freedom Technique)

Support, newsletters, free download of the basic manual.

www.emofree.com

BSFF (Be Set Free Fast)

Another simple and effective meridian therapy.

www.besetfreefast.com

TFT (Thought Field Therapy)

The original meridian therapy.

www.tftrx.com

TAT (Tapas Acupressure Technique)

A slightly different method, possibly involving the use of the Underlying Happiness state. It's not exactly a meridian therapy. Effective for allergies, and works on generational traumas. The website offers a free online tutorial. We don't yet know if the results ever reverse.

www.tat-intl.com

TIR (traumatic Incident Reduction)

A regression therapy that uses the 'viewing' principle. The results are not reversible, as they can occasionally be with meridian therapies. See also Gerald French and Chrys Harris, *Traumatic Incident Reduction*, New York, CRC Press 1999, 174 pp.

www.tir.org

EMDR (Eye Movement Desensitization and Reprocessing)

This power therapy is probably the one most accepted by mainstream psychologists. See, also Francine Shapiro and Margo S. Forrest, *EMDR: The Breakthrough Therapy*, 1998; or the more recent *Eye Movement Desensitization and Reprocessing: Basic Principles, Protocols and Procedures,* 2nd edition, by Francine Shapiro, PhD (Guildford press, 2001).

www.emdr.org

Image Streaming

This is not a therapy per se; rather, it is a set of tools to improve inner vision and creativity. We use it to help people get images in regression, and learn to recognise the information that they do perceive.

www.winwenger.com

Bibliography

Aldana, Jacquelyn, *The 15-Minute Miracle Revealed,* Inner Wisdom Publications, 2003.

Brennan, Barbara Ann, *Hands of Light*, New York: Bantam Books, 1988, 281 pp.

Craig, Gary, *EFT: The Manual*, 1999, 79pp.

French, Gerald D., and Chrys Harris, *Traumatic Incident Reduction,* Boca Raton: CRC Press, 1999, 164 pp.

Grog, Stanislav, *Realms of the Human Unconscious*, New York: Viking Press, 1975, 255pp.

Grof, Stanislav, *The Adventure of Self-Discovery*, Albany: State University of New York Press, 1988.

Grof, Stanislav, *The Cosmic Game*, Albany: State University of New York Press, 1998, 268pp.

Hendricks, Gay, *The Learning to Love Yourself Workbook,* New York: Simon and Shuster, 1990, 188 pp.

Hendricks, Gay, *Learning to Love Yourself: a Guide to Becoming Centered*, Prentice-Hall, 1987.

Hendricks, Gay, and Kathlyn Hendricks, *At the Speed of Life*, New York: Bantam, 1993, 320 pp.

Janov, Arthur, *The New Primal Scream*, Wilmington, DE: Enterprise Publishing, 1991, 372 pp.

Janov, Arthur, *The Anatomy of Mental Illness,* Berkeley, CA: Berkeley Pub Group, 1977.

Joy, W. Brugh, *Avalanche*, New York: Ballantine Books, 1990, 334pp.

Lewis, Thomas, Fari Amini and Richard Lannon, *A General Theory of Love, Vintage, 2001, 230pp.*

Maslow, Abraham, *Religions, Values, and Peak Experiences*, New York: Penguin Books, 1976.

MacLean, Paul, *The Triune Brain in Evolution*, New York: Plenum Press, 1990.

McFetridge, Grant, and Mary Pellicer, *The Basic Whole-Hearted Healing Manual, 3rd Edition, ISPS* Press, 2004, 259 pp.

McFetridge, Grant, *Peak States of Consciousness: Theory and Applications Volume 1*, ISPS Press, 2004, 315 pp.

Index

E

F

G

H

I

J

L

Y

Z

Lightning Source UK Ltd.
Milton Keynes UK
UKHW030223090920
369569UK00008B/1667